Judgment According to the Deeds

Christian Heritage Rediscovered

The Series, as the name suggests, is meant to focus on Christian Faith & Living vis-à-vis topics like Literature & Poetry, Indigenous Philosophizing, Ethical response towards Agriculture, Health & Healing, Science & Technology, Ecofeminist Theology, Sociological approach towards Human Rights, Law & Politics, Arts, History of Ideas, Ancient Civilizations, Cultural Contiguity, Religious Cosmologies & Mysticism, Footsteps of famous Theologians, World Peace & Harmony, Global Capitalism, Network Marketing, Cybertheology, Population & Demographics, Epigraphic Studies, Contextualized Education, and many others. We welcome a Mss. on any topic/s mentioned, whether they are original works, scholarly monographs, collections of conference papers, revised dissertations, or translations of historical documents. Through the Series we, the Publishers, are striving to put forward published works that may help Institutions, Academic Bodies, Researchers, Scholars and the World at large in furthering their respective knowledge and understanding on the concerned subject. We welcome your comments on our efforts and further suggestions on how we can foster the upcoming thoughtful theologically grounded books.

Christian Heritage Rediscovered - 24

Judgment According to the Deeds

An Appraisal of Article X of the Presbyterian Church of India's Confession of Faith

Laldingluaia

CWI

Christian World Imprints(TM)

First Published in 2015 by

Christian World Imprints™
Christian Publishing & Books from India
H-12 Bali Nagar, **New Delhi-110015**
info@christianworldimprints.com
www.ChristianWorldImprints.com
Phone: +91 11 25465925

ISBN 13: 978-93-5148-080-8 (HB) ISBN 10: 978-93-5148-081-5 (PB)

Cataloging in Publication Data--DK

Courtesy: D.K. Agencies (P) Ltd. <docinfo@dkagencies.com>

Laldingluaia, 1976- **author.**
Judgment according to the deeds : an appraisal of article X of the Presbyterian Church of India's confession of faith / Laldingluaia.
pages cm. -- (Christian heritage rediscovered ; 24)
Includes bibliographical references (pages).
ISBN 9789351480808 (HB)
ISBN 9351480815 (PB)

1. Justification (Christian theology)--Biblical teaching. 2. Judgment--Biblical teaching. 3. Eschatology. 4. Lushai (Asian people)--India--Mizoram--Religion. 5. Mizoram (India)--Church history. 6. Presbyterian Church of Mizoram--Creeds. 7. Presbyterian Church of India--Creeds. I. Title. II. Series: Christian heritage rediscovered ; 24.

DDC 234.7 23

Printed at D. K. Fine Art Press Pvt. Ltd.

The Book

The Presbyterian Church of India's Confession of Faith Article X deals with the doctrine of the Last Day. Its main theme is the resurrection of the dead and the subsequent "final judgment" where the living and the dead "shall be judged according to the deeds done in this present life." But the understanding and interpretation of the word "shall be judged according to the deeds" has often been held in tension with the basic theological principle of the Reformation, namely, "justification by grace alone through faith."

Beside this tension it poses, Article X is silent upon important eschatological themes like the immediate state of the dead, the second coming of Christ and millennialism which were major concerns of Mizo Christians soon after they embraced Christianity. The main focus of the Article X thus seems to be the impending judgment according to one's deeds on the Last Day. Taking all these into account, this book seeks to analyse the concept and the nature of "shall be judged according to the deeds" in Article X.

Asserting the interrelatedness of the concepts "judgment according to the deeds" and "justification by grace alone through faith," this book explores the biblical and theological background, and analyses the contextual understanding, of the concept of "judgment" in the afterlife and seeks its implication for shaping the present eschatological imagination of the Mizo Presbyterian Church in particular, and the wider Presbyterian families in India in general.

The Author

Rev. Laldingluaia is an Ordained Minister of the Presbyterian Church of India, Mizoram Synod, teaching Christian Theology and Ethics at the Aizawl Theological College, Aizawl, Mizoram. Prior to that assignment, he had been fully engaged in pastoral ministry in rural context both in and outside Mizoram for a number of years. His areas of interest include the theology of Augustine and John Calvin, Christian eschatology, theological hermeneutics and the interface of science and theology.

List of Abbreviations

A.D.	*Anna Domini*
AICS	Academy of Integrated Christian Studies
ATC	Aizawl Theological College
BC	Before Christ
BCE	Before Common Era
BCM	Baptist Church of Mizoram
BMS	Baptist Mission Society
cf.	compare
CSC	Calvin Study Centre
ed., eds.	editor, editors, edition, editions
et al.	and others
ISPCK	Indian Society for Promoting Christian Knowledge
MTLC	Mizo Theological Literature Committee
PAI	Presbyterian Alliance of India
PCI	Presbyterian Church of India
p., pp.	page, pages
rev.	revised
SIUC	South India United Church

SL&PB	Synod Literature and Publication Board
SPB	Synod Publication Board
trans.	translated
UCNI	United Church of North India
UID	Unique Identification
vol.	volume
WCC	World Council of Churches

Foreword

I am delighted to write a brief note about the book, *Judgment According to the Deeds* as found in the Article X of the Presbyterian Church of India (PCI) Confession of Faith.

One of the author's basic interest in this book is a construction of relevant doctrine of the Christian Hope or Eschatology for the contemporary Mizo Christians. In his critical studies of the phrases 'judgment according to the deeds' in the doctrine of the Christian Hope as found in Article X of the PCI, he argued "the final judgment basing on the deeds done in the present life can be, on the one hand, a hope for an open acquittal of believers who, though not perfect, live a life of obedience to Christ, and on the other hand, the condemnation of the unbelieving and wicked who shall suffer punishment due to their sins". He finally concluded that "a relevant eschatology for Mizo Christians cannot be limited to its root in the past – be it confessions or traditions. Due to the growth of knowledge through higher education coupled with the ease of interconnection and dissemination of information, current scientific perspectives of the cosmos must be especially taken into account. This will help Mizo Christian imagination to transcend its narrow confinement which tends to connect every local event with eschatological signs of the times. This openness to scientific perspectives must be maintained in a healthy relationship with the Christian hope which focused on the promises of God in Jesus Christ that will be actualized through the power of the Holy Spirit".

In the Presbyterian Churches across the world, confessions of faith are the hub of the church life and ministry and thus Presbyterian theology is largely a confessional theology. Working on the Reformed principle of *theologia reformata et semper reformanda*, the author critically studies the Confession of Faith of the Presbyterian Church of India, particularly Article X concerning the doctrine of the Christian Hope, acknowledging its historical situatedness and challenging its validity in the new and ever changing context. The book will certainly be a resourceful and enlightening reading not only for those who want to study the faith and the life of PCI but also for those who are engaging in the struggle to integrate faithfulness to tradition and openness to new voices from the context.

The author, Rev. Laldingluaia is an ordained minister of the Presbyterian Church of India, Mizoram Synod, who has been teaching Christian Theology at the Aizawl Theological College since 2014. Prior to that assignment, he had been fully engaged in pastoral ministry in rural context both in and outside Mizoram for more than seven years. While studying B.Th and B.D at Aizawl Theological College, he was adjudged as the best student securing two coveted Senate Prizes in History of Christianity and Christian Ministry. Later in his M.Th studies at the United Theological College, Bangalore, he proved to be one of the brightest students of Christian Theology under the Senate of Serampore College (University) securing First Class in the Senate final examination, 2014.

Rev. Laldingluaia is one of the most promising Mizo theologians, who will be making a substantial contribution both for the Church and society in the years to come.

Rev. Dr. H. Vanlalauva
Formerly Principal & Professor
of Aizawl Theological College, Aizawl (1998-2007) &
Dean of the Department of Research/SATHRI,
Senate of Serampore College, Serampore (2011-2014).

Acknowledgements

This book in its original form is my thesis submitted to the Senate of Serampore College (University) in fulfillment of the requirements for the degree of Master of Theology and published with written permission. I am responsible for the title, contents and opinions expressed in it.

With a deep sense of gratitude, I wish to acknowledge the help and contributions of the following:

My supervisors, Rev. Dr. Allan Samuel Palanna, Professor of Theology and Ethics, United Theological College, Bangalore and Rev. Dr. Hubert Manohar Watson, Professor of Theology and Ethics, Karnataka Theological College, Mangalore who encouraged and helped me constantly with their invaluable inputs for my M.Th thesis, which is the basis of this book.

My professors, Rev. Dr. Joseph Prabhakar Dayam and Rev. Dr. R. Sahayadhas who helped me to see the possibilities as well as the problems of this particular area of research when I first planned to write on it.

Rev. Lalawmpuia Hauhnar, Registrar, United Theological College, Bangalore for the immense support and the vital "brainstorming sessions".

My classmates at United Theological College, Bangalore, who were my "dialogue partners" as we embarked on our theological journey which sometimes seemed like a "desperate hope".

Rev. Dr. H. Vanlalauva, the former Principal of Aizawl Theological College, who influenced and shaped my theological outlook, for encouraging and inspiring me continuously, and for giving his precious time to write a "Foreword" to this book. I especially want to acknowledge the insights I draw from his book, "Hun Hnuhnung Thu" (Eschatology) which is, in my view, one of the finest books written in Mizo that deals with the diverse "eschatological issues" among the Mizo Christians.

Rev. Dr. Lalsawma, Rev. R. Lalthanmawia and Revd. Chuauthuama for their generous suggestions and guidance.

The Mizoram Presbyterian Church Synod for supporting me financially in my theological journey.

My publisher Christian World Imprints, especially Mr. Sudhanshu Kanda and his team for their suggestions and most skilful assistance throughout this enriching process.

My parents and family, for their ceaseless words of encouragement and prayer.

Saidingpuii Chhakchhuak for going through the draft despite her busy schedule.

My wife R. Lalchhanhimi and my two sons Calvin and Caleb, for gracefully and patiently bearing the stressful weight of my research work.

Above all, I give thanks to God for the gift of a living hope.

Contents

Chapter 1

The Presence of the Future: The Present for the Future

Rejoice, young man, while you are young,
and let your heart cheer you in the days of your youth.
Follow the inclination of your heart and the desire of your eyes.
But know that for all these things God will bring you into judgment.
Ecclesiastes 11:9

Fascination with the future of humanity, society, the world and even the cosmos is not a recent phenomenon. We are amazed by the future and excited by the mystery of what might happen next. In their desire to know and even control future events, people turn to astrologers who insist that events on the earth are connected to the motions of the planets across the sky. Fortunetellers make predictions through crystal-gazing, cards and palm reading while prophets and visionaries warn people about the impending doom. Futurologists anticipate scientific and social changes by analyzing existing trends and forecasting the "possible" or what could happen, the "probable" or what would likely happen, and the "preferable" or what should happen, in the future. Whatever the reason may be, with varying degrees of significance, there is no denying that the future has such a hold on the present.

Of course, one thing we can be sure about this intriguing future is the certainty of death. And this is where religion comes in. According to Lynne Rudder Baker:

> Death comes to all creatures, but human beings are unique in realizing that they will die. Hence, they are unique in being able to consider the possibility of life after death. Ideas of an afterlife of one sort or another have been promulgated by all manner of cultures and religions...Far from being a matter of wish fulfillment, an afterlife, as pictured by ancient cultures, was not particularly desirable, just inevitable. There are many conceptions of an afterlife. To say that there is an afterlife (of any kind) is to say that biological death is not the permanent end of a human being's existence.[1]

If there is an afterlife, usually considered to be in the realm of the infinite future, what kind of life will it be? What will determine the life of the afterworld? Can the present life have any implication for the afterlife? This book is an attempt to look at the answers that Christianity gives to these existential questions. The book specifically explores the Mizo Christian understanding and interpretation of the word "shall be judged according to the deeds" as implied in Article X of the Presbyterian Church of India's (hereafter referred to as PCI) Confession of Faith. The book also seeks to define the Mizo Christian attempt to incorporate these answers into their daily life and the tension it creates in their understanding of salvation.

1.1 The Tension Between the Present and the Future: Justification Now, Judgment Later?

The PCI's Confession of Faith contains ten articles that deal with the doctrine of the scripture, God, the Trinity, creation, Christology,

1 Lynne Rudder Baker, "Death and the Afterlife," in *The Oxford Handbook of Philosophy of Religion*, ed. by William J. Wainwright, (Oxford: Oxford University Press, 2005), p. 366.

the Holy Spirit, soteriology, sacraments, duty of believers and finally, eschatology. Article X, in particular, states:

> At the last day the dead shall be raised and all shall appear before the judgment seat of Christ and shall be judged according to the deeds done in this present life whether good or bad. The unbelieving and wicked, being condemned, shall suffer the punishment due to their sins, but those who have believed in Christ and obeyed Him shall be openly acquitted and received into glory.[2]

But the understanding and interpretation of the word "shall be judged according to the deeds" in Article X is sometimes held in tension with the basic theological principles of the Reformation, namely, "justification by grace alone through faith." The doctrine of justification deals with the question of what an individual has to do in order to be saved.[3] For John Calvin, whose theology greatly shapes the Presbyterian traditions till today, justification depends upon the grace of God and is received through faith alone:

> [W]e explain justification simply as the acceptance with which God receives us into his favor as righteous men (sic). And we say that it consists in the remission of sins and the imputation of Christ's righteousness.[4]

So, Calvin asserts the futility of good works for justification:

> [F]avor with God is not obtained by anyone through works. [T]here never existed any work of a godly man (sic) which, if examined by God's stern judgment, would not deserve condemnation; [and] if such a work were found…it would still

2 *The Constitution of the Presbyterian Church of India*, 7th rev. ed., (Shillong: The Presbyterian Church of India, 2004), p. 4. Hereafter cited as *Constitution of the Presbyterian.*

3 Alister E. McGrath, *Christian Theology: An Introduction,* 4th ed., (Malden: Blackwell Publishing, 2007), p. 372. Hereafter cited as McGrath, *Christian Theology.*

4 John Calvin, *Institutes of the Christian Religion* III.11.2, trans. by Ford Lewis Battles, (Philadelphia: The Westminster Press, 1960), p. 727. Hereafter cited as Calvin, *Institutes.*

> lose favor - weakened and stained as it is by the sins with which its author himself is surely burdened.[5]

This reformation watchword of "justification by grace through faith alone" is also the theological heritage of the PCI, the Welsh Calvinistic Methodist Church being their "mother church".

But in explicating this article, i.e., Article X of the PCI Confession of Faith, when judgment according to one's deeds is reckoned to imply "reward," it is often held in tension with the understanding of "justification by grace through faith alone". And when so much stress is put on "deeds" and the ensuing reward, "salvation" seems to be gained through one's merit. On the other hand, some interpretation leans so heavily on "salvation by grace through faith alone" that good works are deemed unnecessary and even seen as an act of faithlessness. The concept that stressed upon indispensability of "grace through faith alone" for the salvation of human being is therefore often held to be incompatible with the concept that one "shall be judged according to the deeds" in the Last Day. This tension often finds expression in the teaching and the theological articulation of the PCI.

Apart from this tension it poses, Article X is silent upon important eschatological themes like the immediate state of the dead, the second coming of Christ and millennialism which were major concerns of Mizo Christians soon after they embraced Christianity. The main focus of the Article X thus seems to be the impending judgment according to one's deeds in the Last Day. Taking all these into account, this book seeks to analyse the concept and the nature of "shall be judged according to the deeds" in Article X and attempts to align it with soteriological issues it entails, and its implication for shaping the present eschatological imagination of the Mizo Presbyterian Church in particular, and the wider Mizo Christians and the Presbyterian families in India in general.

5 Calvin, *Institutes* III.14.8,11, pp. 775, 778.

1.2 Imagining the Past, the Present and the Future as One Reality

In investigating the biblical, historical and theological basis for the concept of judgment according to one's deeds in the Last Day and examining whether the Article X adequately addresses diverse eschatological issues that concern Mizo Christians, the research was conducted through literary reviews and interviews with selected persons. The outcome was analysed and interpreted using the "hermeneutic of imagination". In this book, the "hermeneutic of imagination" did not connote an elaborate and complicated "methodology" but simply asserted that imagination helps us to interpret and understand reality, which in turn shapes our world views.

In proposing imagination as a key to understand reality, I draw inspiration from Garrett Green's book *Theology, Hermeneutic and Imagination* where Green describes how the modernists understand imagination as a source of speculation, fantasy, and illusion, unless it remains securely subjected to critical reasons. As "imagination" is totally opposed to "reality", modernists who assume that religion is the product of imagination also assert that religious claims are untrue. Green then points out how post-modernity discards the modernists' "foundational" assurance that they have

> reliable access to a "reality" against which imagination might be judged "illusory." Imagination now becomes the unavoidable means of apprehending "reality," though there is, of course, no guarantee that it will succeed….An intellectual culture that thought it had achieved access to secure, secular foundations for human knowledge and behavior...is giving way to a culture that acknowledges that all data are theory-laden, all theories based on paradigms, all knowing dependent on imagination. In short, the postmodern sensibility acknowledges that the use of reason not only does not oppose, but necessarily entails, some kind of faith.[6]

6 Garrett Green, *Theology, Hermeneutics, and Imagination: The Crisis of Interpretation at the End of Modernity*, (Cambridge: Cambridge University Press, 2004), pp. 13-6.

Therefore, I believe that in exploring the socio-religious imagination of pre-Christian Mizo and the eschatological imagination of Mizo Christians, the subjects investigated were not just pure speculations or illusions but a fusion of horizons between a faith-molded reality and reality-inspired faith.

Using "imagination" as hermeneutical tool also demands discretion. Green notes that "the systematic ambiguity of imagination with regard to truth is what makes the concept so useful, and at the same time so treacherous, for theology."[7] K. L. Hughes also states, "While the flourishing use of the human imagination is an asset to theological thinking…one must ask what controls or disciplines this imagination?"[8] And John Polkinghorne, who believes that one form of exploring theological truth is to use imagination "to pursue a theme beyond the point of firmly based knowledge," also warns of the apparent "danger of succumbing to phantasy" in the process and of the "error to attempt to claim certainty where it is not to be had."[9]

So, I ascribe three aspects or dimensions to imagination as essential to Christian theology: the past, the present and the future. Imagination is grounded in the past and shaped by revelation, tradition and experience in religion. Imagination also tries to make sense of the present by looking towards the future and focusing on the goal. In looking towards the goal, imagination inspires one to live out the present in anticipation of the end. These three dimensions were understood as intrinsically interrelated, forming part of a holistic vision of reality- a triune vision. And this "perichoretic" vision of reality does not consist of just a literal reaffirmation of the past imagination. Not limited to a reassertion of what God did in the past, but through faith in Jesus Christ by the power of the Holy

7 Garrett Green, "Imagining the Future," in *The Future as God's Gift: Exploration in Christian Eschatology*, ed. by David Fergusson and Marcel Sarot, (Edinburgh: T&T Clark Ltd., 2000), p. 75.

8 Kevin L. Hughes, "The Crossing of Hope, or Apophatic Eschatology," in *The Future of Hope*, ed. by Miroslav Volf and William Katerberg, (Michigan: William B. Eerdmans Publishing Co., 2004), p. 106.

9 John Polkinghorne, *Exploring Reality: The Intertwining of Science and Religion*, (New Haven: Yale University Press, 2005), p. 169.

Spirit, it is open to the future, thereby admitting the provisionality of the present imagination.

1.3 Scope, Limitation and Structure of the Book

Although the Confession of Faith of the PCI is professed by Presbyterians living in different parts of India, the book limits itself to the context of Mizoram. Although some themes concerning the Last Day have been mentioned as a passing reference in some Articles of the PCI Confession, the book confines itself to Article X. The main focus of the book is the eschatological implications of judgment though it overlaps with themes like soteriology and Christology. And presupposing that most Mizo Christians believe in the "last/final judgment", the research focuses on the concept of judgment as professed in the Presbyterian Church's tradition and evaluates it in the light of the popular Mizo understanding and interpretation of eschatology.

At this juncture, I must briefly introduce the Mizo. The Mizo are the people living in and around Mizoram which is located in the north-eastern part of India bordering Myanmar and Bangladesh. *Mizo* is an umbrella term of various clans who, by and large, adopted the *Duhlian* dialect spoken by the *Lusei* clan. Formerly known as the *Lushais* by the British colonialists, the Mizo settled in and around Mizoram, (literally "Mizo land") from pre-historic time. Before the arrival of the British who colonised them in the late 19th century, the Mizo were leading semi-nomadic lives characterised by an egalitarian society. Before they became Christians as a result of Western missionaries who worked among them from the last part of the 19th century, they were regarded as animists. From being a part of Assam as *Mizo District* after the independence of India, Mizoram became a full-fledged State in 1987. The majority of the Mizo are members of the PCI. Generally, Mizo Christians can be considered as "evangelical" in their theological stance. "Eschatological issues" permeated their worldview, often resulting in dissension and the emergence of sectarian groups.[10]

10 For an introduction to the Mizo and their religion, see Zairema, "The Mizo Church," in *Ground Work for Tribal Theology in the Mizo Context*, ed. by Rosiamliana Tochhawng, K. Lalrinmawia and L.H. Rawsea, (Delhi: ISPCK,

There are four subsequent chapters in this book. Chapter two is an overview of the concept of "judgment according to the deeds" in the Bible and the early Church, and the problems that this concept poses today. Chapter three asks why eschatology matters so much for Mizo Christians and traces how the pre-Christianity Mizo were influenced by belief in reward and judgment in the afterlife, and how that belief influences Mizo Christian spirituality. Chapter four explores the theological and historical background of the Article X and its main theme "judgment according to the deeds" in order to see its original meaning and its alignment with soteriological questions. Chapter five is a general appraisal of Article X where the significance of "judgment according to the deeds" is drawn for, and used to critique the present context.

2007), pp.16-8; Vanlalchhuanawma, *Christianity and Subaltern Culture: Revival Movement as a Cultural Response to Westernisation in Mizoram*, (Delhi: ISPCK, 2006), pp. 9-14.

Chapter 2

The Concept of "Judgment According to the Deeds": An Overview

Many of those who sleep in the dust of the earth shall awake,
some to everlasting life,
and some to shame and everlasting contempt.
Daniel 12:2

This chapter is an overview of the biblical concept of "judgment according to the deeds" which gave rise to the concept of "the Last Day". It also highlights the development of these concepts, later branded collectively as "eschatology",[1] among the early Christians

1 According to G. Sauter, the term "eschatology" stems from Abraham Calov's dogmatic work in 1677. Calov entitled the final section of his work that "deals with the 'last things' specifically death and the state after death, the resurrection of the death, the last judgment, the consummation of the world, hell and everlasting death, and finally, life everlasting" as *eschatologia,* thus the term. Gerhard Sauter, "The Concept and Task of Eschatology: Theological and Philosophical Reflections," *Scottish Journal of Theology*, 41/4, (Nov. 1988), p. 499.

and looks at some of the problems that traditional eschatology poses for the postmodern sensibility.

2.1 The Old Testament's Concept of "Judgment According to the Deeds"

The Hebrew word *shaphat* and its cognate form *mishpat* are generally translated as "judgment", "to judge", and "justice." According to Leon Morris, *shaphat* is basically "the process whereby one discerns between the right and the wrong and takes action as a result."[2] *Shaphat* is also an aspect of God's sovereignty and the result of God's righteousness.[3] Nichols states, "God's judgment is a consequence of God's justice; to deny judgment would be tantamount to denying that God is just."[4] So, judgment and justice are inseparable and justice is expected whenever judgment is carried out.[5]

J. Arthur Baird states that there are three major ways in which *shaphat* is used to describe the action of God in relation to human. Firstly, the word describes God acting as a judge where the action or the outcome of the action is reward or punishment, a blessing or a curse (Ps 75:7). Secondly, the word describes God acting in judgment to punish and condemn (Ezek 25:11). Thirdly, the word describes God acting in judgment to defend, vindicate and save. (Ps 72:4). Baird further notes two consequences of God's judging activity: the necessity for doing something to avoid God's condemnation and to merit God's favour, and the possibility that human being may choose to obey and disobey this divine requirement.[6]

It was asserted that this concept of responsibility and accountability, which is closely linked with the idea of "covenant",

2 Leon Morris, *The Biblical Doctrine of Judgment*, (London: The Tyndale Press, 1960), p. 17. Hereafter cited as Morris, *Biblical Doctrine of Judgment.*

3 J. Arthur Baird, *The Justice of God in the Teaching of Jesus* (London: SCM Press Ltd., 1963), p. 41. Hereafter cited as Baird, *Justice of God.*

4 Terence Nichols, *Death and Afterlife: A Theological Introduction*, (Michigan: Brazos Press, 2010), p.161. Hereafter cited as Nichols, *Death and Afterlife.*

5 Richard Schultz, "Justice," in *New International Dictionary of Old Testament Theology and Exegesis,* Vol.4, W. A. VanGemeran, (gen.ed.), (Carlisle: Paternoster Press, 1996), p. 839. Hereafter cited as Schultz, "Justice".

6 Baird, *Justice of God,* p. 41.

had a "transgenerational corporate" nature until the exilic period (ca.605-538/7 BCE). But, post exilic prophets voiced a new sense of individual accountability and affirmed that individuals are not judged for the iniquities of their ancestors but only for their own.[7] And the belief that the righteous should be rewarded by prosperity and the wicked punished by misfortune in this life was often negated by life experiences. So, the notion of a just and omnipotent God required "an eschatology which promised that the justice of his dealing with individual men and women would be vindicated after death, since too often it was not demonstrated in this life."[8] Tracing this eschatological development, Bauckham says:

> Hope for eternal life beyond death was a remarkable development in Israelite/Jewish faith in the Second Temple period. At the beginning of that period, in the late sixth century BCE,...most Jews retained the old Israelite idea that the dead exist as shades in the underworld (Sheol) [which is] a place of darkness and silence, from which no one returns....They are the dead, in a silent, dark, joyless - indeed, deathly - existence, cut off from God, the source of all life.[9]

It was believed that the Book of Daniel envisaged an ultimate act of divine deliverance involving both living and dead Israelites while the recognition that all would not deserve such deliverance led to the related belief in a final judgment (Dan 12:1-2).[10] It developed into a world view, branded as "apocalypticism," that was marked by the hope that God will soon intervene "into human history to save his people and punish their enemies by destroying the existing cosmic order and by restoring or recreating the cosmos to its original

---

7 Eliezer Segal, "Judaism," in *Life after Death in World Religions*, ed. by Harold Coward, (Delhi: Sat Guru Publications, 1997), p. 16. Hereafter cited as Coward, *Life after Death.*

8 S. G. F. Brandon, *The Judgment of the Death: The Idea of Life after Death in the Major Religions,* (New York: Charles Scribner's Sons, 1967), p. 63. Hereafter cited as Brandon, *Judgment of the Death.*

9 Richard Bauckham, *The Jewish World around the New Testament,* (Tubingen: Mohr Siebeck, 2008), p. 245.

10 Brandon, *Judgment of the Death,* pp. 65-7; Segal, "Judaism," in Coward, *Life after Death,* p. 18.

pristine perfection."[11] In reviewing the apocalyptic writings of that period, Wright states that resurrection is God's act of "firmly setting the world, and Israel, to rights after the long years of earthly injustice and even the longer years in which the righteous have waited, after death, for final vindication."[12] So, the concept of a just and omnipotent God who judged with righteousness culminated into belief of a God who will reverse the present world order and pass judgment according to one's deeds in the resurrection of the dead.

2.2 The New Testament's Concept of "Judgment According to the Deeds"

In the New Testament, the Old Testament concept of divine judgment and justice is expanded further. John the Baptist announced the nearness of God's approaching judgment and stressed the need to repent and be baptized so as to attain God's forgiveness and amends one's life (Matt 3:7-10). Jesus proclaimed a similar call to repentance due to the seriousness of sin and of the divine judgment on it (Matt 5:22-30). This demand for repentance emphasizes the judgment of individuals, though the social and communal responsibility is not overlooked.[13]

The Greek word *krino*, and the cognate words *krinein*, *krisis* and *krima,* which were translated as "to judge", "judgment", were often used for God's present activity of judging.[14] According to Baird:

> [O]f the 112 occurrences where God is the subject of the judgment, [hu]man is always the object, the issue is always a moral one, and the result is generally linked with the future destiny of [hu]man...There is [also] a considerable heightening

11 David E. Aune and Eric Stewart, "From the Idealized Past to the Imagery Future: Eschatological Restoration in Jewish Apocalyptic Literature," in *Restoration: Old Testament, Jewish, and Christian Perspectives*, ed. by James M. Scott, (Leiden: Brill, 2001), p. 148.

12 N. T. Wright, *The Resurrection of the Son of God*, (Minneapolis: Fortress Press, 2003), p. 159.

13 Schultz, "Justice," p. 845; Leon Morris, *Biblical Doctrine of Judgment*, p. 49.

14 Leon Morris, *Biblical Doctrine of Judgment*, p. 45.

> of the negative [aspect of judgment that the words] become really synonyms for condemnation.[15]

In the Synoptic Gospels, Jesus not only preached about the judgment of God but also teached about the judgment of the "Son of Man" which is regarded as his self-designation.[16] And the Johannine Gospel makes it even more explicit that Jesus came into the "world for judgment" (John 9:39; cf. 3:19;5:25-29). So, Higgins asserts that "Jesus confidently expected vindication of his mission after his death by being given, in the presence of God, a status of exaltation that involved the judgmental functions traditionally associated with the apocalyptic Son of man."[17] Similarly, Baird states:

> In his actions, as in his teaching, Jesus performed the disturbing, shocking, abrasive task of bringing men to judgment.... [placing] himself in the very judging position of God, not only within history but at the *eschaton* as well...[in his] own self-estimate he is, in a strangely definitive way, the expression, the instrument, the criterion, and indeed the very incarnation of the judgment of God.[18]

In short, we can say that the rest of the New Testament mostly considered Jesus - the risen and coming Christ, as the one who judged and will judge. The only ambiguity lies upon what the basis and the nature of this judgment will be. According to Brandon, the Gospels which were meant for the Greek-speaking Jewish Christian communities were influenced by Jewish apocalyptic traditions and

15 Baird, *Justice of God*, p. 59.

16 O'Collins notes three context where Jesus use the "Son of Man" for his self-designation: his earthly work and its humble condition (Mark 2: 10, 28; Matt 11:19; 8:20); his coming suffering, death, and resurrection (Mark 8: 31; 9: 31; 10: 33-4); his future coming in heavenly glory to act with sovereign power at a final judgment (Mark 8: 38; 13: 26-7; Matt 24: 27; Matt 25: 31-2). Gerald O'Collins, *Christology - A Biblical, Historical and Systematic study of Christ*, 2nd ed. (Oxford: Oxford University Press, 2009), p.63. Baird also noted that out of a total of 43 occurrences, the phrase "Son of man" 17 times refers to the judge at the *eschaton*. Baird, *Justice of God*, p. 249.

17 A. J. B. Higgins, *The Son of Man in the Teaching of Jesus*, (Cambridge: Cambridge University Press, 1980), p. 1.

18 Baird, *Justice of God*, p. 249.

therefore, usually envisaged a post-mortem judgment where the verdict would be decided by the individual's own action or inherent nature (Matt 25:41-5; cf. Matt 5:29-30). This conception also shaped the *Revelation to John* in which the divine judgment to come is the vindication and avenging of the martyrs (Rev 6:9-10). [19] John Guckin observes that the central theme of the Book of Revelation is the belief of God's execution of "judgment over the world through his Christ. The martyrs demand redress at the heavenly throne (6:10;16:7;18:24) and the heavenly liturgy celebrates this redress given in the divine judgment (15:3-4;19:1-2). The works of human are the criteria of their judgment."[20]

Brandon also argues that this Jewish-Christian perception of the basis and nature of the "Last Judgment" was altered by Paul when he preached to the Gentiles. In interpreting the Crucifixion of Christ, Paul saw the whole of humankind in a state of perdition and only through the death of Christ, and not by their own moral effort, could they be saved from eternal damnation. By accepting Christ as Lord and Saviour and being baptized, the convert was spiritually reborn and incorporated into the Risen Christ and was saved, thereby entering into eternal life (Rom 5:12-6:11). As salvation is God's gift that one must receive in faith, Paul addressed the issue of judgment on the basis of deeds by insisting that fruit of the Spirit will be manifested in the lives of the believers (Gal 5:22-3), who will either be rewarded or suffer loss according to the way they live out their Christian lives (1 Cor 3:10-15; cf. 2 Cor 5:10). [21] Therefore, this passage is to be seen "within the larger framework of Paul's doctrine of justification."[22]

19 Brandon, *Judgment of the Death,* pp. 101-4.

20 John A. McGuckin, "The Book of Revelation and Orthodox Eschatology: The Theodrama of judgment," in *The Last Things,* ed. by C.E. Braaten and R.W. Jenson (Michigan: Wm. B. Eerdmans Pub. Co., 2002), p. 115. Hereafter cited as Braaten and Jenson, *The Last Things.*

21 Brandon, *Judgment of the Death,* pp. 105-7; Leon Morris, *Biblical Doctrine of Judgment*, p. 67.

22 Joseph A. Burgess, "Rewards, but in a very different sense," in *Justification by Faith: Lutheran and Catholics in Dialogue VII*, ed. by H. John Anderson, et al., (Minneapolis: Augsburg Publishing House, 1985), p. 104.

Another factor influencing the concept of "judgment according to the deeds" was the receding expectation of an imminent return of the Lord so that attention shifted to the transitory period between death and resurrection. Terence Penellum observes that the pre-Christian belief that every person

> would be judged at death and would then be with God or cut off from God reasserted itself....[So] the emerging expectation is of two judgments: an individual one at death, to be followed by a universal judgment, or judgment of the nations, at the close of history...[As there is] no room for these two judgments to give different verdicts for the same individual, (so) one or the other becomes something of a formality.[23]

Thus, "judgment according to the deeds" in the New Testament was a diverse concept that was shaped by the complex situation of the early Christians. While an aspect of Jewish eschatology which suggests judgment in a cataclysmic end-time was retained, the existential need of believers in between the present and the end time also envisions a decisive judgment immediately after death or even in this life.

2.3 The Concept of "Judgment According to the Deeds" in the Early Church

Although the New Testament's witness to the notion of "judgment" was not consistent, the concept of Christ as the judge became significant in the developing Christology of the early church. Studying the "Christian apocrypha" of the first two century, B.E. Daley observes that

> the dramatic sense of crisis and the powerfully imaginative expectation of a wholly new order of space and time...bear close resemblance to the Jewish apocalyptic literature...The distinctive element is the role of the glorified Christ as executor of the judgment of God and divinely sent inaugurator of the new age.[24]

23 Terence Penellum, "Christianity," in Coward, *Life after Death*, p. 40.

24 Brian E. Daley, *The Hope of the Early Church: A Handbook of Patristic Theology*, (Cambridge: Cambridge University Press, 1991), p. 9. Hereafter cited as Daley, *Hope of the Early Church*.

Daley also states that apart from Irenaeus,[25] Clement of Alexandria[26] and Origen,[27] most of the writings of the third and early fourth century reflected the apocalyptic hope of Christians as they lived in the midst of social alienation and persecutions.

> Popular expectation of an immediate end of the world seems to have reached fever pitch...Christian writers concerned themselves more and more to reflect ordinary people's beliefs about the afterlife, and used popular expectations of future reward and punishment as an instrument for reinforcing their own social and moral message....The sufferings which the Church underwent seemed, within their own perspective, strikingly like the woes traditionally predicted for God's people at the end of time.[28]

Thus, Christian writers stressed the future reward and punishment to support their message and Cyprian was particularly known for stressing the "greatness of the reward promised those who remain faithful in adversity."[29]

After Constantine granted freedom of worship to the Church in 313 A.D., a large numbers of Christians retreated to deserts from a now-friendly civilized world to purify their commitment to Christ by "voluntary martyrdom". They were motivated by the "traditional

---

25 Irenaeus envisioned "a grand, continuous conception of salvation-history, whose final achievement lies in the not-too distant future." Daley, *Hope of the Early Church*, p. 29.

26 According to Daley, "Clement tends to conceive of the Christian life in terms of painstaking development rather than of eschatological crisis and decision.... In the Paedagogos,...Clement portrays the resurrection of the body as the final realization of human 'enlightenment'. [He interpreted] all punishment, including punishment after death, as purification rather than retribution." Daley, *Hope of the Early Church*, pp. 44, 46-7.

27 According to Daley, "Origen tends...to emphasize the continuity between the present Christian life and its eschatological *telos* or goal, to assume that eschatological statements must have a present as well as a future relevance, and to see the fundamental historical pattern of all creation - cosmic and individual - as one of free, yet providentially guided growth towards union with God." Daley, *Hope of the Early Church*, p. 48.

28 Daley, *Hope of the Early Church*, pp. 33-4, 65.

29 Daley, *Hope of the Early Church*, p. 41.

expectations of judgment, reward and punishment after this life, as well as a vivid conception of the spiritual drama of death itself."[30] There was also a shift in the concept of judgment from a general to a personal event. So, while the Nicene Creed and the Apostles' Creed pointed to a final collective judgment, some of the writings of the Church fathers contain dramatic portrayal of belief in judgment of individual souls.[31] John Chrysostom's depiction is a typical example: "Our actions, our words and our thoughts will be placed in the scales, and the dip of the balance on either side will carry with it the irrevocable sentence".[32]

Augustine, who organized the "early Christian hope" and integrated them "into a broad theological synthesis that is both philosophical and scriptural, speculative and pastorally practical"[33] had been a great influence on eschatology even today. Though we find various references to "judgment" in Augustine's writings, book twenty of *The City of God* was specifically dedicated to an "Argument—Concerning the last judgment, and the declarations regarding it in the Old and New testaments."[34] Though we cannot give a detailed treatment of Augustine's work here, we can say that this book, beside the Bible, contains the essential elements upon which later concepts were developed and classified in systematic theology as "eschatology".

So far, we have been looking at the development of the concept of "judgment according to the deeds" from the Old Testament period till it was systematized by Augustine in the 5th century. From a positive affirmation of God's justice that hoped for an act of divine

---

30 Daley, *Hope of the Early Church*, p. 69.

31 Brandon observes that beyond affirming belief in resurrection and judgment of the dead, the church never attempted to define its teaching on eschatology as thorough as it dealt with the issue of the Trinity or the nature of Christ. Brandon, *Judgment of the Death.* p. 114. This may be due to the end of persecutions.

32 Brandon, *Judgment of the Death,* p. 122.

33 Daley, *Hope of the Early Church*, p. 131.

34 Augustine, *The City of God,* translated by Marcus Dods, 3rd Printing Hendrickson Publishers Edition, (Massachusetts: Hendrickson Publishers, Inc., 2011), p. 641.

deliverance, there was a gradual shift in the notion of "judgment" which lay much stress upon the negative aspect that it became almost synonymous with punishment and condemnation. In later chapters, we shall see how the concept of "judgment" and the related notion of "the righteousness of God" posed a problem in the Christian understanding of salvation. But now, we shall briefly sketch some of the problems posed by the concept of "judgment according to the deeds" in a postmodern context.

2.4 Problems Regarding the Concept of "Judgment According to the Deeds"

2.4.1. Traditional Christian eschatology and modern biblical scholarship: Asserting belief in "judgment according to the deeds" based on biblical account and traditional Church confessions presupposed a number of suppositions that one can find problematic today. The basic problem includes belief in the second coming of Christ, and its related concept of life after death and the resurrection of the body, the interim state of the dead before the final judgment and the outcome of the final judgment. Thus, Pannenberg observes that the history of modern biblical exegesis was marked by "a long history of critical dissolution of the eschatological conceptions exhibited in the Bible" that dismissed biblical eschatology as relying upon an outdated cultural condition, and on a limited knowledge of natural process.[35] R. B. Hays also contends that many Christians consider all the ideas about the second coming of Christ in the Last Day as "quaint speculations that should be shed by mature, educated believers."[36]

And this development led some scholars to compromise between naïve acceptance and outright rejection of biblical eschatology by proposing "realized eschatology" and "existential eschatology." Realized eschatology was proposed by C. H. Dodd who argued that

---

35 Wolfhart Pannenberg, "The Task of Christian Eschatology," in Braaten and Jenson, *The Last Things*, p. 3.

36 Richard B. Hays, "Why do you Stand Looking Up Toward Heaven?" in *Theology and Eschatology at the Turn of the Millenium*, ed. by James Buckley and L. Gregory Jones, (Malden: Blackwell Publishers Ltd., 2001), p. 114. Hereafter cited as Hays, "Why do you Stand…"

the "last things" that Jesus preached have actually happened in his ministry or has been realized in the life, death and resurrection of Jesus Christ. And Bultmann interpret eschatology existentially by arguing that human beings were forced to make existential decisions when faced with the reality of their own death. For him, "judgment" does not refer to some future event of divine judgment but the present event of our own judgment of ourselves, based upon our knowledge of what God has done in Christ.[37] Accordingly, "eternal life" means a different quality of life here and now,[38] and "judgment according to the deeds" was largely understood as part of an outdated biblical concept or, at best, something that has "already taken place whenever anyone hears the gospel and responds either in faith or in unbelief".[39]

The concept of a "final judgment" also needs to deal with the question regarding the double outcome of this "judgment" that presupposed the final separation between "the saved" and "the damned" who will end up in heaven and hell respectively. Highlighting the problem with this traditional view, Moltmann writes:

> Why did God create human beings if he is going to damn most of them in the end, and will only redeem the least part of them? Can God hate what he himself has created without hating himself? If salvation or damnation depends on a person's faith and righteousness, is God not then making his Judgment dependent on the will of human beings, thus really making himself dispensable? [40]

2.4.2. Postmodern secular culture and the uncertainty of the future: The critical stance of modern biblical scholarship toward biblical eschatology was escalated by the postmodern culture which lacks "a

---

37 McGrath, *Christian Theology*, pp. 472-4.

38 Peter Vardy, "A Christian Approach to Eternal Life," in *Beyond Death: Theological and Philosophical Reflections on Life after Death*, ed. by Dan Cohn-Sherbok and Christopher Lewis, (London: Macmillan Press Ltd., 1995), p.13.

39 Hays, "Why do you Stand..." p. 116.

40 Jurgenn Moltman, *The Coming of God: Christian Eschatology*, trans. by Margaret Kohl (London: SCM Press Ltd, 1996), pp. 239-40. Hereafter cited as Moltman, *Coming of God*.

promising image of an authentic future."[41] According to Webster, "Post modernism simply abandons the whole task of making sense: protology and teleology, and agents with stable or developing identities, are renounced, and history is dismantled into a jumble of heterogenous bits."[42] Encouraging individuals and communities to rely solely on their own creative insight and discourse, postmodernity rejects any effort to "discern patterns of meaning in the monument of the past that might shed light on contemporary experience."[43] This rejection of a meta-narrative was evident in Mark Taylor's critique of the Western concept of history:

> Between the "tick" of Genesis and the "tock" of Apocalypse, the history of the West runs its course. The line that joins beginning, middle, and end traces the plot that defines history. History, as well as self, is a theological notion.[44]

Reflecting upon this postmodern worldview, Miroslav Volf and Katerberg argued that optimism of modern period has given way to a sense of ambiguity and they state:

> The biblical tradition, precisely that resource from the past to which Christians must take recourse in order to address the present culture of ambiguity, makes less and less claim on our contemporaries because it is ignored, forgotten, or rejected, or manipulated and marketed by its proponents.[45]

Besides, naturalism or materialism asserts that nature, or matter, is all that really exists while modern cosmology can allot

---

41 Braaten and Jenson, "Preface," in *The Last Things,* p.viii.

42 John Webster, *Word and Church: Essays in Christian Dogmatics*, (Edinburgh: T&T Clark Ltd, 2001), p. 270. Hereafter cited as Webster, *Word and Church.*

43 Paul D. Hanson, "Prophetic and Apocalyptic politics," in Braaten and Jenson, *The Last Things,* p. 47.

44 Mark C Taylor, *Erring: A Postmodern A/theology*, (Chicago: The University of Chicago Press, 1984), p. 53.

45 Miroslav Volf and William Katerberg, "Retrieving Hope," in *The Future of Hope*, ed. by Miroslav Volf and William Katerberg, (Michigan: Wm. B. Eerdmans Pub. Co., 2004, pp. ix,x.

no physical space for heaven or hell in the universe.[46] Thus, the increasing skepticism undermines belief in the afterlife and leaves little room for a concept of "judgment according to the deeds," and even of God. This secular mentality and its sense of ambiguity may be best exemplified by Dawkins words:

> In a universe of blind physical forces and genetic replication, some people are going to get hurt, other people are going to get lucky, and you won't find any rhyme or reason in it, nor any justice....DNA neither cares nor knows. DNA just is. And we dance to its music.[47]

2.4.3. The quest for certainty in the midst of ambiguity: This postmodern sensibility has had important implications for Christian eschatology. Since unifying truth is denied *a priori* as a category, it is argued that one interpretation or reconstruction is as good as any other.[48] The sole validity or primacy of the biblical concept of "judgment in the Last Day" is questioned as belief in an afterlife in different religions do not "necessarily involved belief that the dead would be judged on the quality of their previous life."[49] Questioning whether we should talk about something universal like a decisive "final judgment", it also challenges the notion of historical time as linear, and thus teleological, because it particularly depends on the worldview of the Judeo-Christian tradition.

And in the face of this pessimistic uncertainty, "lost individuals are desperate to find certainties, and they quickly fall prey to fundamentalism...[and people] in search of meaning flock to sects that offer absolute truths."[50] Described as a "meaning system"[51] in

---

46 Nichols, *Death and Afterlife*, pp.11-2.

47 Richard Dawkins, *River out of Eden: A Darwinian View of Life,* (London: Weidenfeld & Nicolson, 1995), p. 133.

48 Paul D. Hanson, "Prophetic and Apocalyptic politics," in Braaten and Jenson, *The Last Things,* p. 50.

49 Brandon, *Judgment of the Death*, p. 5.

50 Paul D. Hanson, "Prophetic and Apocalyptic politics," in Braaten and Jenson, *The Last Things,* p. 48.

51 From a psychological perspective, Hood, Hill and Williamson make an observation that "the meaning fundamentalists derive from their religious

the midst of ambiguity, fundamentalism[52] within Christianity holds the inerrancy of Scripture, bodily resurrection and pre-millennialism as three of the six fundamental tenets.[53] We shall later see how this fundamentalism actually poses a problem among the Mizo Christians with regard to the understanding of eschatology in general and the understanding of "judgment according to the deeds" in the Last Day in particular.

Conclusion

In this chapter, we have taken a look at the biblical concept of "judgment" which was rooted in the justice of God and saw how it inspired a faith that looks beyond this world, to the future, in the hope for a final vindication. We have seen how this faith-inspired worldview, expressed in the traditional eschatology, was often dismissed as a relic of the past in the secular postmodern world. We also made a passing reference to how fundamentalism, which can partly be considered as the counter-product of modern and postmodern ambiguousness, posed a problem today. In a sense, we

beliefs is what allows them to persevere in an inhospitable culture: It creates a way for them to interpret the world, as well as themselves in relation to the world. This meaning system encompasses all of life and is strongly felt, for it deals with issues of eternal importance. It also provides a framework for motivation, and in the process helps meet several personal needs for meaning, such as purpose, value, efficacy, and self-worth." W. Paul Williamson, Ralph W. Hood, Jr., and P. C. Hill (eds.) *The Psychology of Religious Fundamentalism* (New York: The Guilford Press, 2005), p. 5.

52 The term was originally derived from a series of pamphlets that a group of orthodox Protestants in the United States published in the early twentieth century under the title "The Fundamentals" in response to a number of social problems of the time, thus referring to themselves as 'fundamentalists'. The fundamentalist label was now imposed upon different religious communities and cultures by outsiders so that 'fundamentalism' has become a general term for a range of rather diverse phenomena. Thus, we speak of Islamic Fundamentalism or "Hindutva" as Hindu Fundamentalism. Gerrie ter Haar and James J. Busuttil, eds., *The Freedom to do God's Will: Religious Fundamentalism and Social Change,* (New York: Routledge, 2003), pp. 2-4.

53 David Wilkinson, *Christian Eschatology and the Physical Universe,* (London: T&T Clark International, 2010), pp. 3-4. Hereafter cited as Wilkinson, *Christian Eschatology.*

can say that the past and the future forcefully collide in the present, leading to an ideological confrontation. In the next chapter, we shall look at the eschatological concept of the early Mizo Christians, the factors which shaped it, and see how the concept of "judgment according to the deeds" was crucial to this worldview.

Chapter 3

Eschatological Concept of the Early Mizo Christians

For in this tent we groan,
longing to be clothed with our heavenly dwelling.
II Corinthians 5:2

In this chapter, we shall see the Mizo Christian understanding of eschatology and the factors shaping this understanding. The chapter will particularly explore the pre-Christian Mizo concept of life after death, marked by a belief in reward and judgment which has greatly influenced their worldview, and has continued to deeply influence Mizo Christian spirituality and eschatology. Besides highlighting the major eschatological themes and concerns of early Mizo Christianity, the chapter will relate the gradual shift in their eschatological imagination, particularly after "discovering" the concept of "justification by faith" – which has a great implication for the present and the future life.

3.1 Pre-Christian Mizo Eschatological Concept

According to Han Schwarz, expecting life beyond was a primal human phenomenon. This expectation was molded largely by the conviction of an immortal figure of the soul. And the concept of the last things, the *eschata* was made by this primal human notion of a soul or spirit. Schwarz believes that this concept of the last things significantly influences the present people, their conduct and their well-being. Thus, he understands eschatology as "a comprehensive, concept extending to this life and beyond."[1] Seen from this perspective, it can be affirmed that the "primal" Mizo had a clear eschatological concept.[2] Believing in life after death, they held that the human soul will go to either *mitthi khua* or *pialral.*[3]

3.1.1. Mitthi khua (abode of the dead): The pre-Christian Mizo concept of life in *mitthi khua* was like a shadowy existence where the souls led a life quite similar to this world with the continuing need to toil to make a livelihood. Quite similar to the Hebrew concept

---

1 Hans Schwarz, *Eschatology*, (Michigan: William. B. Eerdmans Publishing Co., 2000), pp. 25-6. Hereafter cited as Schwarz, *Eschatology.*

2 Here, "primal" Mizo indicates the sum total of the traditional pre-Christian Mizo before they adopted a more "sophisticated" worldview of the Christian religion. In this sense, the researcher agrees with Lalsangkima who argues that Mizo Primal religion did not dichotomize between sacred and profane, but that the entire socio-cultural life was an expression of their religion and religiosity. Lalsangkima Pachuau, "Mizo 'Sakhua' in Transition – Change and Continuity from Primal Religion to Christianity," *Missiology: An International Review,* 34/1, January, 2006, p. 42. Hereafter cited as Sangkima, *Mizo Sakhua*.

3 There may be an exception as Lalsawma notes that the souls of those who were a nuisance to the community, and those who were disobedient to their parents were believed to wander in the cliff and dense forest, and turn into ghosts and demons. Lalsawma, "Mizo Pialral Thurin leh Chanchin Tha," in *Kristian Thurin Zirna*, (Aizawl: SL&PB, 1998), p. 305. Hereafter cited as Lalsawma, *Kristian Thurin Zirna.* Zairema also notes that an adulteress was considered an easy prey of the tiger, and that her soul was held in servitude by the tiger. Therefore, *em mawng pawp* (closely-woven basket without a bottom) was put in her grave so that she can carry the prey of the tiger, the reason being that as the basket was without bottom, the meat can fall out and hence, will never be too heavy. Zairema, *Pi Pute Biak Hi*, ed. by Chhuauthuama (Aizawl: Zorun Community, 2009), p. 122. Hereafter cited as Zairema, *Pi Pute Biak Hi.* It may also be that this servitude occurred in *mitthi khua* of the spirit world.

of *Sheol*, their miniature and surreal existence at *mitthi khua* was evident from things ascribed to the dead: firefly/glow worm was identified with the dead soul, their "bear" a hairy worm and their "fish" a dry leaf.[4]

3.1.2. Pialral (abode of the blessed): Situated on the other side of *mitthi khua*, *pialral* [5] can be an equivalent of "paradise" for the Mizo where the souls led an idyllic existence. It was believed that in *pialral*, there was plenty of ready-to-cook husked rice.[6] Though they do not describe the nature of the place, to lead a life where they do not need to toil and labour in contrast to the hardship they face to earn their daily livelihood is the ideal life in the pre-Christian Mizo imagination. Lalsawma noted that while there was no indication of a desire to go to *mitthi khua*, *pialral* is a place which everybody aspired for.[7]

3.1.3. The final destiny of the soul as judgment: Before leaving the world for the spirit world, the soul lingered for about three months in the vicinity of the village, and then departed toward the spirit world at the request of his/her family. The soul had to proceed toward the final destiny, taking one of the seven paths that converge at *Pu Pawla kawtchhuah* (Pawla's gate/pass) called *Zingvawnzawl*, where the road to *mitthi khua* and *pialral* diverge again. There resided *Pu Pawla* and his wife *Sanu*, whose house could not be passed by anyone without crossing a large stone so slenderly balanced that the noise would bring *Pu Pawla* out of his house, pellet-bow in hand. Except those who were on their way to *pialral*, anyone who passed by was shot with his fierce egg-size pellets which could inflict a painful tumour/wound

4 Lalsawma, *Kristian Thurin Zirna*, p. 303. cf. Zairema, *Pi Pute Biak Hi*, p. 136.

5 Literally meaning "beyond the *Pial*", *Pial* either denotes a river on the otherside of *mitthi khua,* or the earth, which is poetically often referred to as *piallei*. Thus, Lalsawma argued that even if there is a river *Pial*, it will literally mean "river earth." Lalsawma, *Kristian Thurin Zirna*, p. 304.

6 J. M. Lloyd, *History of the Church in Mizoram*, (Aizawl : SPB, 1991), p. 14. Hereafter cited as Lloyd, *History*.

7 Lalsawma, *Kristian Thurin Zirna*, p. 304.

lasting three years to heal.[8] Thus, being chased by the showering pellets of *Pu Pawla* toward *mitthi khua* where the soul would lead a melancholic existence can be considered a dreadful "penal judgment" in the pre-Christian Mizo eschatological imagination.

3.1.4. Entitlement to Pialral: There are four groups of souls which *Pu Pawla* would not shoot. Firstly, infants who died before they reached three years of age, as what they would have become is not known; secondly, virgin girls and virgin women; thirdly, young men who lay with either three virgin girls or seven women; fourthly, *thangchhuah* couples, on whose sight *Pu Pawla* and *Sanu* hid in terror. Of these four, *pialral* is categorically entitled by *thangchhuah* couple while the other groups may also pass safely to *pialral.*[9]

The title *thangchhuah* can be attained in two ways - *ram lama thangchhuah* and *in lama thangchhuah*. The former title was given to a man who killed specified number of different animals in the chase and making public celebrations of the kills. This required a man to kill animals such as a bear, a sambhur, a barking dear, a wild boar, a wild mithun, an elephant, a poisonous snake called *rulngan*, a flying lemur and a species of eagle called *muvanlai*. The latter title was given to a man who can give a certain number of grand public feasts in sequence. The wife of such a man also shared his title.[10]

3.1.5. Implication of 'Pialral' and 'Thangchhuah' for the present life: Sangkima observes that the traditional Mizo "beliefs and practices were impelled by the strong communal value system of the society, and could not be isolated from everyday affairs of the community."[11] In the light of this observation, important questions arise as to why the theology of *pialral* developed, why *thangchhuah* were categorically entitled for *pialral* and what it implied for the

8 Lloyd, *History*, p. 14; Zairema, *Pi Pute Biak Hi*, pp. 133-135.

9 Lloyd, *History*, p. 15; Zairema, *Pi Pute Biak Hi*, pp. 137-139; Lalsawma, *Kristian Thurin Zirna*, pp. 305-6.

10 Zairema, *Pi Pute Biak Hi*, p. 60; J. H. Lorrain, "Thangchhuah," in *Dictionary of the Lushai Language*, (Calcutta: The Asiatic Society, 1940), p.447. Lloyd notes that the list of animals required to attain *ram lama thangchhuah* differs from place to place and from time to time. Lloyd, *History*, p. 15.

11 Sangkima, *Mizo Sakhua*, p. 42.

present life. In analyzing the requirements for *ram lama thangchhuah*, Zairema points out that most of the animals that were to be killed to attain *thangchhuah* were in fact pests that destroyed their paddy fields and crops. While it was already tough to cultivate and protect one's plot, hunting and chasing implied sacrificing one's time and energy to ward off these animals for other's sake. And the meat of the game were not theirs alone but was to be shared by the whole community. Upon that was the requirement of making public celebrations of the kills.[12] So, all these requirements acknowledged and encouraged a selfless community service.

And in analyzing the requirements for *in lama thangchhuah*, Zairema believes that behind its promises of *pialral* there may have been an underlying desire to uplift the poor. *Thangchhuah* people were held in high-esteem because of their generosity to the needy. Due to ill-health some families might not reap enough rice for a year. So while preparing for the grand occasion of *in lama thangchhuah*, very often they scooped their rice from the rice-bin and slopped on the floor purposefully or spilled it from their mortar while pounding the rice. The spilled rice was collected by the poor. Besides assisting the needy and treating the community with the 'finest rice and tastiest meats' they also gave away their valuables.[13] Lalthangliana also believes that the high-water mark of the Mizo religion is not *pialral.* For the road to *pialral* demanded social service through providing the needy and uplifting them, risking and sacrificing one's life for the sake of others and for social security against beast and foes. Thus he remarks that there is a "vertical dimension" as well as a "horizontal dimension" in the Mizo religion.[14] And Sangkima opines that these requirements were prescribed "to suit the societal needs.... to be a blessing to the entire community."[15]

12 Zairema, *Pi Pute Biak Hi*, pp. 144, 171.

13 Zairema, "Kristian Nih Hmaa Mizo Sakhua," in *Mizo Miziaa Pathian Thu: Mizo Kristian Theology Kawng Zawnna*, (Aizawl: SPB, 1988), pp. 45-46; Zairema, *Pi Pute Biak Hi*, p. 171.

14 B. Lalthangliana,"Mizo Sakhua," in *Pi Pu Chhuahtlang*, (Aizawl: Hrangbana College, 1998), p. 219.

15 Sangkima, *Mizo Sakhua*, pp. 43, 46.

Therefore, we can clearly see a blend of the present and future world, the individual achievers and the benefiting community, as the motif of *thangchhuah* and *pialral*. The present need for survival and self-sacrifice, productivity and communal sharing was encouraged by emphasizing the future reward of individuals displaying gallantry and the ability to produce surplus food. As one's deeds and merits in this world was the basis for judgment and reward in the afterlife, the principle guiding Mizo eschatology is that "life in this world becomes key factor in determining the status of life after death."[16] So, pre-Christian Mizo eschatology are not simply things that take place at the end but rather things which had started in this world and had powerfully shaped their world views and values in this life.

Therefore, we can say that judgment and reward motif was already present in pre-Christian Mizo eschatology. Accordingly, the Christian concept of "judgment according to one's deeds" was not an alien concept for the Mizo when they hear the Christian messages. In the next section, we shall see how this pre-Christian Mizo eschatology was incorporated with the Christian message and how the Mizo responded to this messages.

3.2 Early Mizo Christian Understanding of Eschatology: The First Decade

Rev. William Williams, the pioneer missionary, reached Aizawl on 20th March 1891 and stayed there for a month. Rev. J. H. Lorrain and Rev. F. W. Savidge who worked under the Arthington Mission reached Aizawl on 11th January 1894. They were joined by Rev. D. E. Jones on 31st August 1897. After the first two missionaries left Mizoram, D. E. Jones was joined by Rev. Edwin Rowlands.[17] Both were under the Welsh Calvinistic Methodist Foreign Mission. They were followed by a number of missionaries at intervals.

3.2.1. The messages of the early Christian missionaries: The early missionaries, influenced by the evangelical awakening and the pietist

16 C. Lalmuankima, *Impact of Westernization on Mizo Spirituality: Implications for the Development of Relevant Christian Spirituality in Mizoram*, (Bangalore: SFS Publications, 2013), p. 138.

17 Lloyd, *History*, pp. 21, 26, 39, 44.

movement in Europe besides having a "triumphant" colonialist outlook,[18] brought the message of "salvation for sinners."[19] But as the Mizo had their own norms and concept of good and bad in community life, and taboos that can be analogous to the concept of "sin", their immediate rebuff was that they were not sinners just because they do not follow "the white men's religion."[20] While their psyche was not impressed initially by the Christian notion of sin and the need for a saviour, the Mizo were anxious not to "transgress" against the evil spirits. For they believe that every illness was caused by evil spirits who can harm them at their slightest displeasure and in order to appease them, costly offerings and sacrifices of animals and crops had to be offered regularly. This anxiety was quickly noticed by the missionaries, as the report sent to the Mission Board in Wales in 1898 by D. E. Jones testified:

> The first difficulty which the Lushai raises against accepting Christianity is the danger that he will be killed by the Evil Spirits, and when it is said that Christians do not become the prey of the Evil Spirits, they say in answer that our religion does

---

18 K. Thanzauva, "Sap Upa leh Pu Buanga-te Historical leh Theological Background," in *Mizorama Missionary Hmasa Ber – F. W. Savidge & J. H. Lorrain* (Tanhril: AICS, 2010), pp. 28-9. Andrew Porter states that in those 'high imperial age', belief in the universality of human nature and the significance of Christianity's message to all humankind was more prevalent among the missionaries than elsewhere. Andrew Porter, "Missions and empire, c.1873–1914," in *The Cambridge History of Christianity, Vol. 8: World Christianities, c.1815-c.1914*, ed. by Sheridan Gilley and Brian Stanley, (Cambridge: Cambridge University Press, 2006), p. 572.

19 Lorrain wrote: "Our first message as soon as we could speak the language, was of a Saviour from sin. But the people had no sense of sin and felt no need for such a savior." J. Herbert Lorrain, "Report for 1913 of the B. M. S Mission in the South Lushai Hills, Assam," in *The Annual Report of B. M. S on Mizoram, 1901-1938*, (Serkawn: Mizoram Gospel Centenary Committee, Baptist Church of Mizoram, 1993), pp. 93-4.

20 Lalsawma, *Kristian Thurin Zirna*, p. 309; C.Lianthanga points out 27 taboos which were regarded an offence against the high God *Pathian*. "Pipu Duh Loh Thilte," in *Hmanlai Mizo Nun*, (Aizawl: Mizoram Publication Board, 1999), pp. 58-61. Cf., Zairema, *Pi Pute Biak Hi*, pp. 141-57.

> for us and theirs for them… Any sickness which they cannot understand is attributed to Evil Spirits.[21]

From the early period of their mission work, the missionaries therefore tried to develop a message to address this concern besides responding to their religious aspirations. According to Lloyd, the substance of the earliest missionary preaching was

> God is good and if you believe in God you will have supreme joy hereafter, and if you don't believe, and persist in your evil ways and adulteries, God will put you among the evil spirits in the everlasting fire and you will endure suffering forever and ever.[22]

And one first-generation-Christian, Zathanga, who later became a Pastor, recalled that the message he first heard from D. E. Jones in 1899 was, "Believe in *Pathian* Jehova and worship him, then you don't need to sacrifice to the demons any more. Even when you die you shall go to *pialral*."[23] According to Grace Lewis, the reason why the missionaries incorporated *Pialral* with the Christian concept of "heaven" may have been due to the deficiency of the Mizo dialect "in its power of expressing abstract ideas...In some instances new significance had to be given words to enable them to convey spiritual meaning."[24] Sangkima also noted that the missionaries learned to preach the Gospel using contextual language and imageries "through their experience of interacting with the people."[25]

---

21 *Reports of the Foreign Mission of the Presbyterian Church of Wales on Mizoram 1894-1957*, compiled by K. Thangzauva, (Aizawl:SL&PB, 1997), p. 4. Hereafter cited as *Reports of FMPCWM.*

22 Lloyd, *History*, pp. 31-2; cf. Lalsawma, "Kristian Thuhril Hmasa Ber," in *Kristian Thurin Zirna*, pp.306-8; C.L.Hminga, *The Life and Witness of the Churches in Mizoram*, (Serkawn: The Literature Society, BCM, 1987), pp. 62-3. Hereafter cited as Hminga, *Life and Witness.*

23 Hminga, *Life and Witness*, p. 62.

24 Grace R. Lewis, *The Lushai Hills: The Story of the Lushai Pioneer Mission*, (London: The Baptist Missionary Society, 1906), pp. 32-3. Hereafter cited as Lewis, *The Lushai Hills.*

25 Sangkima, *Mizo Sakhua*, p. 48. The contextualization of the Gospel was evident from the account of Pastor Liangkhaia who, as a lad, remembered how

3.2.2. Effects of the messages of the early Christian missionaries upon the Mizo: These simple messages had three important implications. Firstly, the Mizo were obsessed by the fear of spirits and demons that can harm them at the slightest displeasure and need appeasement by sacrificial worship. The missionaries tried to assert the superiority of the Christian God over those dreaded spirits and demons by arguing that Mizo sacrifice are "worthless in the sight of God,... [who] is greater than all such spirits. Whoever worships [God] has no need of a sacrifice. God will heal him, for God alone can heal."[26] E. L. Mendus records one incident during a journey when he came across a group of men who cling to their traditional belief for fear of demons:

> When I told them that God was much powerful than the demons and that Jesus Christ, when on earth, actually cast them out of men, I could see that the effect was instantaneous for surprise was so evident in their face.[27]

Thus, the authority of God over evil spirits "touched on a sensitive and vulnerable point in Mizo life,"[28] and had a calming effect on their spirit-infested turbulent life and made the Gospel highly appealing.

Secondly, another "fear factor" that the missionaries took into their advantage was the fear invoked by their preaching upon the Christian doctrines of judgment and hell, which was not an alien concept to the early Mizo because of their eschatology. Mendus stated that this message "has doubtless played a significant part in arousing the people from indifference and sensual torpor."[29] And from his interview with the first generation Christians in 1975, Hminga noted that many of them became Christian for fear of *hremhmun* which

---

D. E. Jones made use of an illustration that becomes very catchy among the Mizo. "He compared the Gospel to the banyan tree. It grows around another tree until the original dies completely. So too the Gospel displaces sin in our hearts when once it begins to grow." Lloyd, *History*, p. 43.

26 As recollected by Pastor Zathanga. Lloyd, *History*, p. 48.

27 E. L. Mendus, *The Diary of a Jungle Missionary*, (Liverpool: Foreign Mission Office, 1956), p. 37. Hereafter cited as Mendus, *The Diary*.

28 Lloyd, *History*, p. 262.

29 Mendus, *The Diary*, pp. 37-8.

literally means "place of punishment", a rendering of the English term "hell", that will be the "fate of the non-believers."[30] Saiaithanga also pointed out that many early converts embraced Christianity for fear of hell.[31]

Thirdly, the message of free entrance to *pialral* (which the missionaries incorporated in the Christian concept of "heaven") for those who believe and obey God's word also meets the religious aspiration of the Mizo as it replaced "the difficult and costly *thangchhuah* as the path to *pialral*."[32] Christianity offered them a better way to "go to heaven" (*vanram kai*) where not only the skillful, the strong and the affluent, but everyone who puts their trust in God has access.[33] Thus, the Christian concept of "heaven" absorbs, fulfills, and in a way surpasses the Mizo conception of *pialral* and reshapes Mizo eschatological imagination.

3.2.3. The stipulations of being a Mizo Christian: The early Mizo Christians were known as *Pathian thuawihho* ("those who were obedient to God").[34] If obedience to God can get them to heaven, an important question is what does "obedience" implied for the early Mizo Christians? What are the requirements they need to fulfill as a sign of their new faith to go to Christian *pialral*, now that *thangchhuah* is obsolete in their new religion? In what way did this shape their values and reflected the eschatological outlook of the missionaries and the Mizo Christians? We need to consider various factors and reconstruct them to determine this.

Firstly, we must take into account the conviction and the vision of the early missionaries who instructed them, as well as their

30 Hminga, *Life and Witness*, p. 62.

31 Saiaithanga, *Mizo Kohhran Chanchin*, 1st edition, (Aizawl: MTLC, 1969), p. 19. Hereafter cited as Saiaithanga, *Mizo Kohhran*.

32 Sangkima, *Mizo Sakhua*, p. 49; thus, Chhuanawma says, "the eschatological concepts of *mitthi khua* and *pialral* found their counterparts in the Christian idea of heaven and hell." Vanlalchhuanawma, *Christianity and Subaltern Culture: Revival Movement as a Cultural Response to Westernisation in Mizoram*, (Delhi: ISPCK, 2006), p. 151. Hereafter cited as Chhuanawma, *Christianity and Subaltern Culture.*

33 Hminga, *Life and Witness*, pp. 62-3, 295.

34 Saiaithanga, *Mizo Kohhran*, p. 24.

sponsors. The first two missionaries, Lorrain and Savidge were sent by Arthington Aborigines or India Aborigines Mission. This mission was financed by a millionaire, Robert Arthington from Leeds, a millenialist with stern evangelical outlook who founded his society in 1889. Arthington was so inspired by his conviction of the urgency of preaching the Gospel to those who never heard it before to hasten the second coming of Christ that he lived in abject poverty.[35] According to Samuel Southall, Arthington

> was fond of telling his friends that he believed it was only necessary for the evangelist to pass through all these tracts of country (as yet untouched by the Truth) distributing Gospels, and preaching the Word, in order that Christ might come and restore all things.[36]

We can assume that the missionaries were chosen, and raring to go, because they held, more or less, the same conviction with Arthington regarding the second coming of Christ. This was even more likely if we consider the writing of Dana L. Robert regarding Christian mission in the last part of the 19th and early 20th century:

> Late nineteenth-century Protestants prayed for and expected revivals….By the 1880s, many devout Christians hoped that a widespread outpouring of the Holy Spirit around the year 1900 would lead to the Second Coming of Jesus Christ,...But first the world needed to be evangelized so that as many souls could be saved as possible before Jesus' return….In order to reach people untouched by the Christian message, [missionaries] moved beyond the established mission stations and into the remote sections of non-Christian parts of the world.[37]

---

35 Chhuanawma, *Christianity and Subaltern Culture,* pp. 97-8.

36 As quoted by Lewis, *The Lushai Hills*, p.35. Before Lorrain and Savidge had been in Mizoram for 18 months, Arthington was already eager that they should move. Lloyd, *History*, p. 32.

37 Dana L. Robert, *Christian Mission: How Christianity Became a World Religion*, (West Sussex: John Wiley & Sons Ltd, 2009), p. 61; cf. Lloyd, *History*, p. 36. At the same time, we must note that Savidge and Lorrain did not conform to Arthington's conviction in every way because they learned the native language and even translated portion of the Bible in Mizo, which Arthington deemed unnecessary because of the limited time and the urgency of the work before

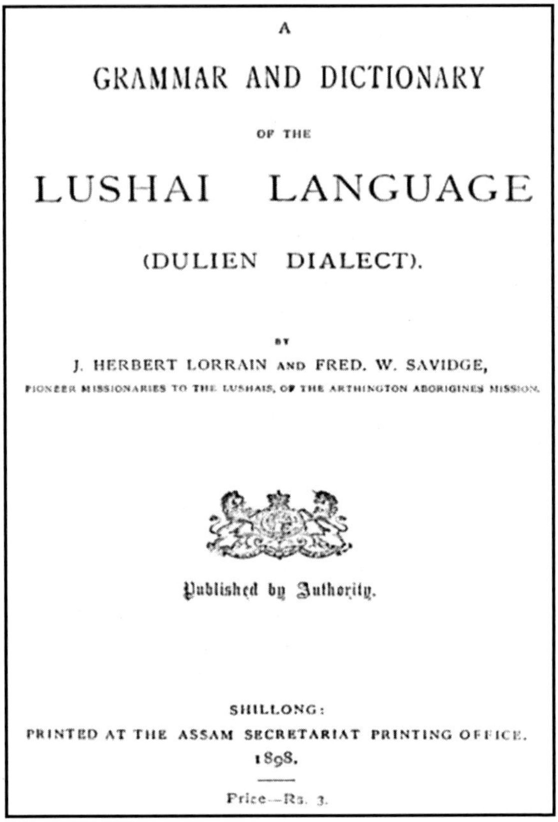

A

GRAMMAR AND DICTIONARY

OF THE

LUSHAI LANGUAGE

(DULIEN DIALECT).

BY

J. HERBERT LORRAIN AND FRED. W. SAVIDGE,

PIONEER MISSIONARIES TO THE LUSHAIS, OF THE ARTHINGTON ABORIGINES MISSION.

Published by Authority.

SHILLONG:

PRINTED AT THE ASSAM SECRETARIAT PRINTING OFFICE.

1898.

Price—Rs. 3.

Fig. 1: The title page of the dictionary made by J. H. Lorrain and F. W. Savidge, the pioneer missionaries of the Arthington Aborigines Mission to Mizoram.

Moreover, the messages preached by the missionaries in the early period are rather eschatological-oriented as they stressed the afterlife and heaven and hell. Saiaithanga observed that this tendency was because 'the end of the world and hell' were dominant themes of Western Christianity during the 19th century.[38] And it can be seen that one of the songs that Lorrain translated in Mizo was "The Lord

the second coming of Christ. For their achievements during their four years in Mizoram, see Chhuanawma, *Christianity and Subaltern Culture,* pp. 101-12.

38 Saiaithanga, *Mizo Kohhran*, p. 19.

is coming by and by, be ready when He comes" while D. E. Jones translated "When the trumpet of the Lord shall sound, and time shall be no more" in Mizo. The eschatological content in these songs is noteworthy.

We can assume that this was also the attitude and conviction of the Welsh Calvinistic Methodist Mission authorities because just before they commissioned D. E. Jones to Mizoram, all their Mission centres in the Khasi Hills and the Sylhet Plain were completely destroyed by the great Assam earthquake in 1897. These heavy losses caused panic and some were reluctant to start new work in Mizoram though the Mission authorities decided to go ahead.[39] Postponement of the work was quite sensible, one can argue, if it was not for their conviction.

Secondly, and related to the above point, is the fact that from the beginning the missionaries stressed the need, and urged the Mizo Christians, to be a self-sustaining, self-supporting church. Early in 1902-03, when there were just a few numbers of Mizo Christians, D. E. Jones reported that they "are endeavouring to introduce the system of tithes here for the support of the work, and are likely, I think to be successful."[40] And we can see how the Mizo Christians made efforts to contribute for supporting the mission work as the reports submitted in 1903-04 and 1905-06 period suggest:

> It was mentioned last year that the system of tithes was being introduced. It has not been without success. Some of the boys give a tithe of their scholarships, and others of their wages, and one gives of his rice.
>
> We were much cheered to understand that the church in Lushai supports four evangelists without receiving any aid from the mission funds. The Christians are taught to contribute a tithe of their earnings toward the cause.[41]

---

39 Lloyd, *History*, p. 38; Lalsawma stated that the early Welsh Mission, just as the "hurrying" Arthington Mission, was also a "hasty mission." Lalsawma, *Kristian Thurin Zirna*, p. 308.

40 *Reports of FMPCWM,* p. 18.

41 *Reports of FMPCWM,* pp. 20, 25. The same practice was encouraged by the missionaries in Southern Mizoram, who reported their "endeavour to make the native Christian Church in this land self-supporting from the first." And the

So, partly due to the financial instability back in Wales, and probably more out of their own conviction about the urgency of evangelization, the missionaries from the beginning encouraged the Mizo Christians to contribute and participate in the mission work.

Thirdly, we must take into account another important stipulation of being a Mizo Christian. Though they wanted quantitative increase in numbers and encouraged new converts to bring others into the fold,[42] the missionaries ultimately wanted qualitative growth. So, they insisted that the converts make a radical break with some deep-rooted traditional practices like giving up drinking of the rice beer, which consequently necessitated the giving up of various religious and social rites.[43] Singing of non Christian songs was discouraged; they should not kill others and must refrain from quarrelling, stealing, lying, and extra-marital relationship and adultery. They must observe Sunday as a day of rest and worship,[44] and most importantly, get rid of the *kelmei* amulet.[45] *Kelmei* is a tuft goat's hair hanging from a string around the neck to ward off evil spirits. As it was believed to protect the wearer, abandoning it was a real sign of intent. When D. E. Jones received *kelmei* from would-be converts, he kept them safe in his office just in case they want it back, and later destroy it if it was not claimed.[46]

---

converts were quite willing that "even before our arrival they had put aside a tenth of their last rice crop." Lewis, *The Lushai Hills*, pp. 51-2. Here, we must note that the practice of paying *fathang*, a tax or tribute to their chief consisting of one or more *dawrawn* baskets (about 15 kgs.) of unhusked rice, may make it natural for the Mizo Christians to contribute tithes.

42 Lalsawma, *Kristian Thurin Zirna*, p. 308.

43 See Saiaithanga, *Mizo Kohhran*, p. 24. Drinking can incur a year suspension from communion. Mendus, *The Diary*, p. 34.

44 Before embracing Christianity, typical Mizo usually worked every day of the week until harvest time, though they observed "public holidays" on occasions like bereavement, religious ceremonies and festivals, public feastings and celebrations. K. Zawla, *Mizo Pi Pute leh an Thlahte Chanchin*, 3rd ed., (Aizawl: H.A. Press, rev. and enlarged, 1981), pp. 142-5.

45 Lalsawma, *Kristian Thurin Zirna*, pp. 307-8.

46 *Reports of FMPCWM*, p. 13; Lloyd, *History*, p. 53.

While adherents and converts were under strict guidelines of the church,[47] new converts also faced many hardships and were even persecuted in some instances. Lloyd said that Mizo preachers "were regarded as daft, as wandering beggars, as lazy layabouts or homeless vagrants" while those who were driven out by the chief of Pukpui from his village formed a Christian village at Sethlun in 1901.[48] And as per the missionary reports submitted in 1900-01 and 1901-02, new converts were compelled to carry loads on Sunday and to give rice to make beer for the feasts. "They have suffered persecution, especially on account of the observance of the Lord's Day.... [O]rder has been given for their removal to another place, on account of their refusal to work on Sunday."[49]

What we can infer from these observations is that the early converts paid a big price in becoming Christians. Beliefs must transpire into action and, like the *pialral* of old, assurance of "heaven", though not earned, largely depends upon their subsequent actions. And considering their eschatological orientation, the missionaries' strong insistence upon right conducts may partly be due to their belief that their labour may soon be tested before the judgment throne of God (I Cor. 3:13). Therefore, the early Christians were instructed to lead an ethical life and were encouraged to contribute their mite and suffer for Christ's sake, as it has an eschatological implication. Even the first song translated from English by a Mizo in 1903, "We shall

47 Lloyd noted that to become Christian, one had to be on probation for at least twelve months, during which he/she had to attend weekly classes to learn the meaning of the Christian faith and had to remove the *kelmei* on one's own free will. Lloyd, *History*, p. 107. This was also evident from a report made in 1901-02, where "several made a start as candidates" in the Bualpui village, "but on account of drink, Sunday labour & c., have gone back," while a report in 1911-12 indicated that several members were lost through death every year, but a larger numbers were lost during that period through expulsion. *Reports of FMPCWM,* pp. 15, 47.

48 Lloyd, *History*, pp. 59, 72; cf. Saiaithanga, *Mizo Kohhran*, p. 24.

49 *Reports of FMPCWM,* pp. 10, 16.

stand before the king" was an exhortation to comply and it had an eschatological overtone:

> Wake, my soul! Thy tribute bring;
> Thou shalt stand before the King,
> By and by, By and by!
>
> Lay thy trophies at His feet;
> In His likeness stand complete,
> By and by, By and by!

3.3 Impacts of Revival Movements on the Mizo Eschatological Imagination

During the next two decades, i.e., 1906-25, Mizoram witnessed three major movements known as "revival" that had greatly impacted Mizo Christian spirituality. Though I had reservation about using the word "revival" to describe these movements, it will nevertheless be used for want of a better terminology.[50] And without describing the socio-political context of these revivals, I shall highlight some important "themes"[51] of these revivals and focus upon the shift in Mizo soteriology during these revival movements which also altered Mizo eschatological imagination ever since then.

3.3.1. The revival of 1906: The revival that came in 1906 had its root in the *Welsh Revival* of the 18th and 19th century.[52] The Welsh revival of 1905 came to Mizoram through delegates from Mizoram attending the Annual Assembly of the Presbyterian Churches at Mairang where a revival was already experienced. This revival

---

50 "Revival" may accurately described the renewal and vigor experienced by Christians belonging to the parent churches in the West, who were previously lethargic and were in a state of slumber after embracing Christianity for so long. But as Mizo Christianity was at its formative or "infancy" stage, I questioned the validity and exactness of using the "label" *revival* for their experiences.

51 For the various "themes" emphasized in these revivals, see Lalsawma, *Kristian Thurin Zirna*, pp. 101-26.

52 These revivals "were characterized by tremendous ecstatic and enthusiastic physical gesticulations and outbursts of joy and prayer." Chhuanawma, *Christianity and Subaltern Culture*, p. 161.

proved to be a milestone in the Mizo understanding of basic Christian messages, for it resulted in the first public experience of sin and the assurance of God's forgiveness.[53] Chhuahkhama, the first ordained Mizo Pastor, stated that Christians, who were usually from the lower rung of the society, began to feel a sense of satisfaction with their present condition in the world. [54] It also stirred a sense of urgency to preach the Gospel and consequently, a number of people were added to the Mizo Christian community. In 1909-10, D. E. Jones gave the following report:

> More were baptized in 1909 than any year since the beginning...One happy way in which it showed itself was in deeply moving many of our Christian school-boys, so that they were constrained to go out far and near to witness for Christ. A large number of heathen [sic]...have handed in their names as desirous of following Jesus....The open confession of Christ in this manner...frequently resulted in persecution.[55]

According to a report in 1911-12, there were 552 communicant members in Northern Mizoram, while the total number in the churches was 1723, with 1800 adherents.[56] This growth was in spite of a setback in the form of persecution, and the appearance of a very popular indigenous song called *Puma Zai*, "the song of Puma" around 1907. Spreading like wild fire, *Puma Zai* was sung and enjoyed over a drink, and celebrating the song with public feasts entitled the celebrant a *thangchhuah* title. It lost its popularity when a famine in 1911 impoverished the people all over Mizoram.[57]

---

53 Chhuanawma, *Christianity and Subaltern Culture,* pp. 158-80; Lloyd, *History*, pp. 86-96; Lalsawma, "Sual leh Chhandamna Thu Mizoram Kristianten an Zirtir Dan," in *Calvina Zirtirna leh Mizo Nun*, ed. by C. Lalhlira, (Aizawl: Calvin Study Center, 2002), p. 147. Here after cited as Lalsawma, *Sual.*

54 As quoted by Saiaithanga, *Mizo Kohhran*, p. 22.

55 *Reports of FMPCWM,* pp. 40-1.

56 *Reports of FMPCWM,* p. 47.

57 Unlike the slow and dirge-like songs sung earlier over a rice beer pot, this song started as a simple lullaby of a double-lined refrain of any number of verses. As new verses were added to this catchy song, it can developed into a powerful mock song that some Christians considered it a "resurgence of heathenism". Chhuanawma, *Christianity and Subaltern Culture*, pp. 180-1,183-4; Lloyd,

3.3.2. The revival of 1913: On the backdrop of this great famine[58], another revival occurred in 1913 that lasted two years. Starting from the eastern part of Mizoram called Hmunhmeltha village, it consecutively spread to various parts of Mizoram. Marked by fervent dancing and singing,[59] Christ's vicarious suffering on the cross captivated their mind and there was a sense of the imminent return of Christ. Lalsawma gives examples that show their haste as the second coming of Christ is imminent: One man distributed all his smoked meat, while another girl distributed all her clothes except the one she wore. One bachelor regretted that he could not marry his fiancée before the end of the world. Others run and preached in haste, urging non-Christians to make up their mind before the time approach.[60] According to Chhuanawma

> the promise of an eternal home where all life's struggles would be consummated by a life of prosperity, which by traditional belief belonged only to the privileged few [make] the theme of Christ's second coming to gather his saints...very attractive to the poverty-stricken public. [61]

This sense of the imminent return of Christ aroused the zeal to preach the Gospel. The zeal to preach the Gospel was evident from D. E. Jones' report for the year 1916-17:

> The Christians in the churches have increased from 7168 to 8579 with a total community of 9315. The number of full

---

History, p. 108. Lalhmuaka stated that they mockingly sang toward the Mizo evangelists preaching in the street as imitators of Western cultures. Lalhmuaka, *Zoram thim ata Engah*, (Aizawl : SPB, 1988), p. 139. Hereafter cited as Lalhmuaka, *Zoram thim ata Engah.*

58 This famine was due to an enormous increase of jungle rats, who fed upon bamboo seeds that flowered the previous year, and after multiplying manifold, consumed most of the standing crops in the jhum the next year.

59 According to Lalsawma, one song was even continuously repeated from Wednesday night to Sunday night. Lalsawma, *Kristian Thurin Zirna*, p.108. The duration of the revival is as per Saiaithanga, *Mizo Kohhran*, p. 48.

60 Lalsawma, *Kristian Thurin Zirna*, p.108. Llyod also noted that this belief "prevented some from sowing the rice in the Spring." Lloyd, *History*, p. 162.

61 Chhuanawma, *Christianity and Subaltern Culture*, p. 201.

> members has increased to 3087,...due to the Revival of 1913, which swept through most of the villages where there were Christians.
>
> The "Soldiers of the Cross,"... have been the means of bringing many to Christ in their own way. These men were supported by friends from home. Beside these, many men,...go about preaching the word in season and out of season.[62]

Chhuanawma believed that this zeal may be largely inspired by Peter Frazer, "the beloved physician" of the Mizo, who held that "Jesus was coming again to judge humans' action in relation to his command." The Mizo Christians "keenly recognized" his conviction.[63]

Another important outcome of this revival movement is the indigenous interpretation and elaboration of the doctrine of Christ's second coming that resulted in the initiation of a sectarian group in Mizoram. It was headed by Tlira who taught that the Second Advent of Christ had already taken place. For him, "The millennial reign and 'rapture of the saints' had taken place through the working of the Holy Spirit. As Christ is the resurrection and the life, those who received Christ through the Spirit were the resurrected ones."[64] This teaching can be considered a radical shift where soteriology was intertwined with 'realized/existential' eschatology and had an important soterio-ethical implication:

---

62 *Reports of FMPCWM,* p. 60. "Soldier of the cross" are bands of unpaid voluntary preachers, almost exclusively men, who tour the land, zealously preaching the Gospel to the remotest part of the land.

63 When the Mission Board asked Fraser why he preferred to work abroad instead of ministering at home, his reply was: "...a distinct and powerful conviction that I am disobeying Jesus by not offering myself for service among the heathen. If I disobey Him in this I know I shall not be able to stand before Him and to hear Him say, 'Why didn't you go?'" Chhuanawma, *Christianity and Subaltern Culture,* p. 201. Saiaithanga stated that Dr. Fraser attended to over fifty thousand patients during his four years stay in Mizoram. Saiaithanga, *Mizo Kohhran,* p. 41.

64 James Dokhuma, *Zoram Kohhran Tualto Chanchin,* rev. ed., (Kulikawn: J. D.Press, 1997), pp. 22-3. Hereafter cited as Dokhuma, *Zoram Kohhran.*

> Sunday should be abolished as all days belonged to God. What is done in the body and by the body cannot affect the Christian's soul; so, one need not worry about their sins. Those who obeyed [Tlira's] teaching were already cleansed.[65]

> [For those who are in Christ] all formalities of the Church such as the Sacrament and the Church's constitution, observation of Sunday are unnecessary or, at best, optional, for those who were heirs with Christ and fellow-citizens with the saints were sharing the reins of eternal judgment with Him.... What was humanly considered a sin like stealing, self-indulging sex and drinking, though best avoided, did not really cause spiritual death and therefore, did not affect one's salvation.[66]

Here, we can detect a trait of body-spirit tension in human being where the spirit was believed to be in bondage in the human body. Tlira's emphasis upon spiritual salvation as opposed to judgment according to one's deeds also represents a radical shift in Mizo Christian soteriology.

3.3.3. The revival of 1919: Within the context of the First World War[67] and the influenza epidemic of 1919 which claimed many lives in Mizoram[68], yet another revival occurred in 1919. Starting simultaneously in three different places on June 26, 1919, this revival lasted for four years and even spread to Manipur and Tripura among kindred Mizo tribes. Seen as the most significant revival in Mizoram, the stress was on the physical suffering and the cross of Christ. Mendus stated that the name of Calvary became better known even than the names of their own hills in those times and "people's hearts were melted by the story of the passion of our Lord

65 Lalhmuaka, *Zoram thim ata Engah,* p. 145; Lloyd, *History*, p. 176; cf. Saiaithanga, who remarked that these "heretics" usually overstressed Apocalytic books like Daniel and Revelation, in *Mizo Kohhran*, p. 49.

66 Dokhuma, *Zoram Kohhran,* pp. 23-6.

67 2100 young men, known as the Lushai Labour Corps, joined the Allied Forces in Frances in 1917. Seventy one of them were lost in action. Chhuanawma, *Christianity and Subaltern Culture*, pp. 231-2.

68 According to Dokhuma, this epidemic was rumoured to claim around 400 lives in some villages in a year, causing great depression that considerably affected the church. Dokhuma, *Zoram Kohhran,* p. 8.

and they were led into an experience of conviction and forgiveness of sins."[69] Saiaithanga also remarked that the theme of the cross, though always captivating to the Mizo, was further endearing to them.[70]

Even more charismatic in nature[71] than the past two revivals, the Mizo drum – previously used to accompany singing in a drinking bout and associated with pre-Christian culture – was introduced into church's worship.[72] Mendus, who reached Mizoram in 1921, recalled his first experience of a revival meeting:

> Benches were removed in order to provide room for those who were dancing, whilst others around me trembled with emotion and swooned away into an unconscious and semi-conscious state which sometimes takes the form of trance.[73]

The drum "created a rhythm to the singing and the dancing [intensifying] the exhilaration of the whole revival movement", and new Christian hymns composed by Mizo using indigenous tunes appeared in succession.[74] According to Thanmawia, around 700 hymns were composed during the year 1920-1936.[75]

Due to this revival, a large number of new believers were added to the Mizo Christian community. In his report given for the year 1919-20, Sandy stated that this revival greatly affected the life of the church and besides being a blessing to those who were already believers, 4000 new believers were added to the church. During the next year the number of Christian was increased by "3699 making a total of 27666 or 29074, counting the hearers" and "wherever there was a revival there was also brotherly love in a marked degree."[76]

---

69 Mendus, *The Diary*, p. 82.

70 Saiaithanga, *Mizo Kohhran*, p. 52.

71 Lalsawma, *Kristian Thurin Zirna*, p. 118.

72 Saiaithanga, *Mizo Kohhran*, p. 51.

73 Mendus, *The Diary*, p. 82.

74 Chhuanawma, *Christianity and Subaltern Culture*, p. 254.

75 R.L.Thanmawia, "Harhnain a hrin hla leh a phuahtute," in *Harhna: Mizoram Revival Centenary Souvenir, 1906-2006*, (Aizawl: Revival Centenary Committee, 2006), pp. 581-4.

76 *Reports of FMPCWM*, pp. 63, 66-7.

On the other hand, there are "many undesirable traits" to this revival:

> Many felt that there was not much religion if unaccompanied by visible signs of emotion – singing, dancing, quaking, swooning.[77]
>
> The emotional element in the revival has taken control of the minds of many....[and] there arises a strong element of insubordination to the authority of the Presbytery and of the Church as a whole. Why, it is asked, obey the voice of man (sic), when we can have immediate access by the Spirit to God Himself.[78]
>
> As time went on some became almost "professional" in their attitude to dancing. It loomed so large in their minds that they could barely tolerate a meeting where dancing took no place. Through dancing they not only participated in the service but exhibited themselves as super Christians and rather despised any who were unable or unwilling to join in.[79]

As this revival movement diminished, there was a backlash to this emotional spirituality,[80] which saw a new theological trend emerging in Mizoram that stressed "salvation by faith" like never before. This began from NE Khawdungsei, a village in the north eastern part of Mizoram. Spurgeon's book, "Advice for Seekers", newly translated as *Spurgeon Sap Thurawn* by H. K. Dohnuna, had been instrumental for its development. Though we cannot get the

77 *Reports of FMPCWM,* p. 67.

78 Mendus, *The Diary*, pp. 82-3.

79 Lloyd, *History*, p. 194.

80 According to Chhuanawma, this emotional and rapturous spirituality earned the displeasure of some influential section of the Christian community which compelled some people, who were also "dissatisfied with the transitory nature of the revival excitement," to look for "a more sober type of awakening." Chhuanawma, *Christianity and Subaltern Culture*, p. 335. Mendus, in his report for the year 1926-27, also wrote that many became Christians or "thought themselves that they were Christians during the Revival. But now when the Revival stopped many of them do not know where they stand; they do not really know what the meaning of Christianity is." *Reports of FMPCWM,* p. 81.

Mizo version of Spurgeon's book, some of his arguments in the original book were that salvation lies in Jesus only and not upon one's doings or feelings.

> This is the universal plan of justification. Faith lays hold upon the righteousness of God, by accepting God's plan of justifying sinners through the sacrifice of Jesus Christ, and thus makes the sinner righteous. Faith accepts and appropriates for itself... divine righteousness.[81]

In 1924, Chhinga, Dengkawnga and Darneihzova, all from that village read this book. Spurgeon's central thesis of "justification by faith alone" persuaded them though they did not profess it openly for fear of being misunderstood. By 1925, they openly proclaimed that an everlasting joy could be found in the experience of free justification by grace through faith alone and their new conviction became an issue of hot debate as opinion differed. So far, the general concept of "salvation" had amounted to saying

> Jesus Christ has redeemed us with his blood. If we believe and serve Him with all our abilities, shunning evil, we will be saved by grace when the sheep and goats are separated before the glorious throne [on the Day of Judgment].[82]

So, they sent for Thangkhuma, the then Pastor in charge and his verdict was that their belief was unfounded, faith lacking deeds and was barren.[83]

During this unsettled differences of opinion, Howard Dinwiddie, the Secretary of the North-East India General Mission came to that village. It appears that the Directors of N.E.I.G. Mission had suspicion that large amount of money meant for missionary work in India and Burma was mismanaged. So, they sent

---

81 C. H. Spurgeon, *Advice for Seekers,* (Edinburgh: The Banner of Truth Trust, 1993, First Banner of Truth Edition), p. 68.

82 Lalruali, *Zoram Hmarchhak Harhna Chanchin*, (Aizawl : SL&PB, 1997), p. 38. Hereafter cited as Lalruali, *Hmarchhak Harhna.*

83 Tlangawia, Chawngchhuanga, Sangthanga, eds., *N. E. Khawdungsei Kohhran Chanchin*, (N. E. Khawdungsei: Presbyterian Kohhran Committee, 1994), p. 70. Hereafter cited as Tlangawia, *et al.*, *Khawdungsei Kohhran.*

Dinwiddie to inspect and on one occasion he came to the village of N. E. Khawdungsei. When matters were brought to his notice he confirmed that "justification by faith" was in line with the teaching of Paul in the New Testament.[84] Soon, "justification by faith" became popular and spread to the surrounding villages and eventually to other parts of Mizoram. "Justification by faith" was ensued by the debate over the doctrine of election and predestination.[85] This new development promoted growing interest in doctrines and biblical teachings. The emerging theological position was that we are saved not by our works and merits. We are not justified by our offerings but faith in Jesus Christ alone.[86] Thus, when the Roman Catholics came to Mizoram in 1926 claiming apostolic succession which implies that outside their fold there is no salvation, "salvation by faith alone" was an instant rebuttal.[87]

On the other hand, it brought along a tendency to downplay Christian duty altogether. As a result, some local churches suffered a drawback in their financial condition. People neglected giving of the tithe (the 1/10th of their paddy harvest) on the ground that merits don't count and are futile for justification.[88] This concern was mentioned in the Missionary reports for the year 1929-30 and 1932-33:

> Because someone had been over-emphasising "Faith" to the detriment of "Works," the collections went down in one part of the country.
>
> There is a great deal of joy in the church, and considerable devotion to the Word of God, accompanied however by rather an alarming interest in such doctrines as Predestination,

---

84 Tlangawia, *et al.*, *Khawdungsei Kohhran*, pp. 70 - 71; Lloyd, *History*, p. 243.

85 According to Lalhmuaka, the doctrine was wide-spread in 1927. Lalhmuaka, *Zoram thim ata Engah,* p. 160. Cf. Lalsawma, *Kristian Thurin Zirna*, p. 4; Lalsawma also states that Liangkhaia was the champion of Calvinism in Mizoram, giving special significance to election and predestination. Lalsawma, *Sual*, p.149.

86 Tlangawia, *et al.*, *Khawdungsei Kohhran*, pp. 69-70.

87 Lalhmuaka, *Zoram thim ata Engah*, p. 160.

88 Tlangawia, *et al.,Khawdungsei Kohhran*, pp.69-70; cf. Lalruali, *Hmarchhak Harhna*, pp. 86-8.

> Election and Justification by Faith…One distressing feature, however, is that the collections do not increase as one would expect.[89]

It also led to an antinomian tendency and neglecting of church's conformity in favour of one's personal spiritual and mystical experience and charismatic fervour. Proper pastoral and theological guidance was often lacking. With little or no idea of the basic elements, people were often caught in the whirlwind of doctrinal debate like, "Who will receive the price of Christ's atonement?" where even the key figures were not consistent.[90]

3.3.4. Mapping the shift in Mizo eschatology: From exploring the typical Mizo Christian eschatology before the revival of 1919, we can make the following remarks–

i. "Judgment and reward" motif was always present in Mizo eschatology: As "judgment and reward" was basic to the theology of *pialral*, every aspect of Mizo Christian eschatology can also be seen in relation to an impending "judgment". So, from the conviction of sin and assurance of forgiveness to the expectation of the imminent return of Christ and the need to hastily preach the Gospel, "judgment and reward" was always basic to Mizo eschatology.

ii. "Judgment and reward" necessitated a tenet: The norm of "judgment and reward" is one's deeds and actions, which in turn influenced one's values in this world. As faith must transpire into action – mainly in conformity with the teaching of missionaries, Christians were willing to toil and even dared persecution for the sake of Christ. On the other hand, those who stressed personal spiritual experience, like Tlira, nullified this tenet and were considered "heretics".

iii. Eschatology is intrinsically connected to soteriology: Any shift in soteriological theme has eschatological implications, for the understanding of salvation - or in some case like Tlira's, how one was "being in Christ" - also determined the understanding of one's

89 *Reports of FMPCWM*, pp. 99, 114.

90 Saiaithanga, *Mizo Kohhran Chanchin*, pp. 54-5; Tlangawia, *et al.*, *Khawdungsei Kohhran*, p. 70.

responsibilities, duties and ultimately, judgment and reward in the "Last Day".

From the revival of 1919 afterward, we can see two major shifts in Mizo Christian eschatology: the first was best exemplified by the theology of the indigenous Mizo hymns while the second was represented by the theme of "justification by faith" and salvation.

i. The theology of Mizo indigenous hymns: Besides the suffering of Christ on the cross, longing for the heavenly home amidst the untold destitution of this world was the dominant theme of these new hymns. Lalsawma remarked that almost all the indigenous songs composed before 1940 rarely missed out on the theme of eschatology and even the most catchy sermons were on the theme of heaven citizenship, the second coming, the great day of judgment and the millennial reign.[91] According to Saiaithanga, this reflected their state of being a poor and hard working people.[92] And as some of those who were expecting the second coming of Christ actually passed away before the moment comes, their bereavement or the possibility of meeting the same fate must make them to contemplate much upon the heavenly home, where the soul of their dear departed ones awaited them. As a result, there is a major shift from a general or cosmic eschatology to personal eschatology. Perhaps Mendus' *Diary* shed light on the people's worldview of the time, and which still holds true even today for many Mizo Christians:

> I have seen people thrilled to the marrow even in times of suffering and grief. I remember one woman at the funeral of her beloved husband actually danced along the edge of his grave from sheer uninhibited joy in the conviction that he was already in a state of heavenly glory in the Presence of his Lord.[93]

---

91 Lalsawma, *Kristian Thurin Zirna*, pp. 310-11.

92 Saiaithanga, *Mizo Kohhran*, p. 54. The first three hymns were *Ka ropuina leh ka himna hmun tur* (There lies my glory and my shelter), composed in 1920 by Patea, *Lei lal puan ropui chu a tlawm ang* (Earthly glories shall fade away) and *Tunah a thar, hmangaihna eng nuamah*, (All thing new before the compassionate light of love) composed in 1922 by C. Z. Huala and R. L. Kamlala respectively.

93 Mendus, *The Diary*, p. 82.

This theology influenced Mizo Christian eschatology so substantially that the resurrection of Christ as the basis of hope, especially if that hope implies bodily resurrection in some remote future, was minimal.[94] The desire to share the "not yet" aspect of eschatology "now" and transcended the sufferings of the world was clearly depicted in this song:

> I persistently long for the place
> Where I will grief no more;
> I am yearning to see the Lord,
> O! Pass away, gloomy earth.[95]

This desire to transcend earthly suffering also posed a tension in terms of the state of the departed souls on one hand, and the second coming and the resurrection of the body and the Last Judgment on the other hand. This tension may resemble the experience of the first-century Christian community as well as those of the subsequent centuries.[96] In this respect, Tyron Inbody observes:

> The early church soon lost its sense of an imminent end. The main stream of Christian thought has retained an idea of a final end, a 'judgment day,' which it puts off into the indefinite future. But what they hope for is that when they die, their soul

94 The lasting impact of this theology is best illustrated by the composition of songs in Mizo Church's hymnary called *Kristian Hla bu*. While there are 148 songs about the person and work of Christ, of which 96 songs are about the love, salvific work and suffering of Christ, only 5 songs were about the resurrection of Christ, of which four were translation. And these five songs mainly reflected upon the resurrection as *Christus victor*, without much implication for the future. And there are 53 songs about heaven and the afterlife. *Kristian Hla Bu*, (Aizawl: SL & PB, 2004), p.vi. This hymn book was further supplemented by the *New Hymnary* whose content were indigenous hymns composed mainly between 1920-40, having an eschatological overtone and stressing upon the desire to transcend this worldly life.

95 L. Kamlova, "Lung min len ka thlir ning dawn lo," in *Mizo Kristian Hla Thar Bu, No. 414*, (Aizawl: SL&PB, 2007), p. 413.

96 See chapter 2.2 for the "tension" in the early church.

> will go to heaven, and they will be prepared to spend eternity in heaven following the judgment day.[97]

ii. Justification by faith and salvation: An important eschatological issue that the debate on justification by faith entailed was regarding assurance of salvation and whether one's salvation can be lost. If one took this position and stretched it, it nullified the final judgment on the Last Day to a certain extent. To its proponents, grace put an end to the law, and judgment must not be based on work and merit. This tension between faith and work was always present from this time onward in Mizo Christian soteriology and eschatology. On the opposite pole are those who equated experiencing of the revival as meritious and assertive of salvation. These "revivalists"[98] stressed emotion to the point where they negate church's authority and teachings as they have direct access to God by the Spirit. Some even deride the concept of the Last Judgment because of their standing before God, considering themselves as actually sharing the reins of eternal judgment now.

But these two extreme views actually converged when the adherents on both sides perceived themselves as "the chosen" or "the elect". These people, because of their "libertine" spirit, often saw the "institutionalized" church as too legalistic and left the church. Their sentiment was clearly expressed in their "Ramthar"[99] songs:

---

97 Tyron Inbody, *The Faith Of The Christian Church - An Introduction to Theology*, (Michigan: William. B. Eerdmans Publishing Co., 2005), p. 304. Hereafter cited as Inbody, *Faith Of The Christian Church.*

98 Here, we must take note of Lalsawma's classification of the "revivalists" into two category: He called the first group "Christians Revivalists" and they constitutes of those people who remain committed to the Christian faith even after the revival fire cooled down. He called the second group "Revival Christian" and they constitutes of those people who switch back to their old way of life after the revival heat passed. Lalsawma, *Revivals: The Mizo Way*, (Mission Vengthlang: Lalsawma, 1994), p. 75. Hereafter cited as Lalsawma, *Revivals: The Mizo Way.* The "revivalists" we referred to here may not fit into these two groups. We can call them "indigenous revivalists" as they wanted to integrate Mizo traditional practice and culture with the Christian message, and usually opposed the "Western" church.

99 Literally meaning "new land" and sung in the indigenous tune, they were popularised by the followers of Tlira and other sectarian groups that can

They said faith was evident in work
But he who heard and kept all the Commandments
Walk away, denied of the Kingdom.

Faith and Work, they make no difference
Faith in Lord Jesus who freely pay the price
Is count as the greatest deeds of all.

There is none to be judge in you
Between Jesus who stood condemned in your place
And the standard of the world, they will decide.[100]

Conclusion

This chapter explores the developing eschatological concept of Mizo Christianity until the mid-1920s, when the Presbyterian Church of Assam adopted a Confession of Faith. This period witnessed the blending of Western theology with traditional Mizo eschatology and its transformation. From being *thangchhuah* enthusiasts, early Mizo Christians became *Pathian Thuawih* to "enter" *pialral* or heaven. In retaining the concept of *pialral* as an "entitlement," the path to *pialral* first demanded conformity to the Christian ethical values and structural organization. Like *pialral* and *mitthi khua* of old, heaven and hell, reward and punishment, were intrinsic to their eschatology. And when judgment was inevitable, life in this world became a deciding factor regarding the status of life after death.

Gradually, after the revival movements, experience of the revival or faith and belief was seen as a key deciding factor in attaining *pialral*, and Mizo Christianity partially became a matter of emotional expression or personal inner conviction of an eternal assurance/

be categorically classified as *Thiangzau*, "the libertines". These songs usually expressed their longing for a new and better land, and are therefore basically eschatological in content. R. L.Thanmawia, *Mizo Hla Hlui (Mizo Folk Songs)*, (Aizawl: Mizoram Publication Board, 2012), p. 588. Hereafter cited as Thanmawia, *Mizo Hla Hlui*. According to Vanlallawma, *Thiangzau* basically advocated antinomianism while few of them leaned toward salvific universalism. C. Vanlallawma, "Sialsuk Pastor Bial Hlimsang Harhna leh a Chhehvel," in *Harhna: Mizoram Revival Centenary Souvenir, 1906-2006*, (Aizawl: Revival Centenary Committee, 2006), pp. 476-8.

100 Thanmawia, *Mizo Hla Hlui*, p. 607.

security through faith in Christ's redemptive work. Perhaps, this may be influenced by pre-Christian Mizo "soteriology" where one was assured a place in *pialral,* once and for all, after fulfilling the *thangchhuah* requirements because there was no concept of a later resurrection. But, understanding and stressing "justification by faith" as a requirement to "attain" heaven can make one to negate Christian duty and service and to become other-worldly. Besides, it marks a radical diversion from pre-Christian Mizo understanding of *pialral* that demanded and encouraged social service, and prompted a tension between faith and work in Christian life.

In the encounter between Mizo and Western eschatology, we see a shift in eschatological concept from a personal to a general/cosmic, and then a purely personal, level. But the idea of "judgment" and "reward" was always central to it. We can also see similarities between the early Mizo Christian community and the early Christian community in the Bible who both went through a transition in their eschatological perspective. In all this, perhaps the most lasting legacy of Western evangelicalism was an eschatology that envisages the resurrection of the dead and the culmination of history in the near future. As this was totally a new concept in Mizo eschatological imagination, the concept of resurrection in particular, causes difficulty in grasping and aligning the notion of "judgment according to the deeds" with "justification by faith."

In the next chapter, we shall see how and to what extent, this Western Christian concept of eschatology, particularly "judgment" in the Last Day, was expressed in Article X of the Confession of Faith of the Presbyterian Church of India. Looking at the theological and circumstantial shifts during the historical process of the drafting of the PCI Confession of Faith, we shall identify the main theme of Article X and see how it was aligned with the concept of "justification by faith".

Chapter 4

Eschatology in the Confession of Faith of the Presbyterian Church of India

See, I am coming soon; my reward is with me,
to repay according to everyone's work.
Revelation 22:12

This chapter will explore how Article X of the Confession of Faith of the Presbyterian Church of India (PCI), which is a confessional statement on eschatology, was formulated. Highlighting the historical development of the PCI, the chapter will look at the factors that influenced the formulation of this Confession. Looking at the biblical and theological basis and the main theme of Article X, the chapter will focus upon the concept of "judgment according to one's deeds" and its alignment with the doctrine of "justification by faith."

4.1 Historical Development of the Presbyterian Church of India

The Presbyterian Church of India traces its beginning to the Welsh Calvinistic Methodist Church, later known as the Presbyterian

Church of Wales, and its missionaries who began their work in the Khasi Jaintia Hills in 1841 and later expanded to the Sylhet-Cachar Plains, the Lushai Hills and the Cachar Hills. In this section, we shall briefly look at the historical development of the Welsh Calvinistic Methodist Church and their missionary enterprise that resulted in the formation and the subsequent development of the PCI.

4.1.1. The Welsh Calvinistic Methodist Church: The Welsh Calvinistic Methodist Church had its origin in the 18th century evangelical revival. This revival can be traced further to the "Holy Club" of the Oxford in the 1730s, which later came to be known as the Oxford Methodist. Regarding the name "Methodist", Charles Wesley recalled that he "went to the weekly Sacrament and persuaded two or three young scholars to accompany me, and to observe the method of study prescribed by the Statutes of the University. This gave me the harmless nickname of Methodist."[1] They were joined by George Whitefield in 1735. During those period, Howell Harris from Trevecca in Wales, also entered one of the college at Oxford but soon after, returned to Wales. Soon, "he ventured to go from house to house, in his native parish, to exhort sinners; and, gradually, he extended his sphere of usefulness to the adjoining parishes also."[2] According to Geraint Tudur, "It was [Howell] Harris's work as a lay evangelist that had first led to a number of conversions among his hearers, and then, in time, to the establishment of societies."[3]

Probing deeper in this regard, Paul Chamber notes that "the new enthusiasm had not emerged from a vacuum" as a network

---

1 Gareth Lloyd, *Charles Wesley and the Struggle for Methodist Identity*, (Oxford : Oxford University Press, 2007), p. 25. Originally, Methodist may be a reference "to some old physicians who were thus called, because they had reduced the science of medicine to method and order." *The History, Constitution, Rules of Discipline and Confession of Faith of the Calvinistic Methodist in Wales*, 2nd ed., (Chester: Parry and Son), 1834, p. 4. Hereafter cited as *The History, Constitution.*

2 *The History, Constitution,* pp. 4-5.

3 Geraint Tudur, "'Thou Bold Champion, Where art Thou?': Howell Harris and the Issue of Welsh Identity," in *Religion and National Identity, Wales and Scotland c.1700–2000*, ed. by Robert Pope, (Cardiff: University of Wales Press, 2001), p. 47. Hereafter cited as Pope, *Religion and National Identity.*

of circulating schools had been started just before the arrival of Methodism, which provided basic literacy and religious instruction for the common people and greatly help the labours of evangelists.[4] He was referring to Griffith Jones, sometimes designated as "the Apostle of Wales," and "the Morning Star of the Methodist Revival,"[5] who work ardently from around 1731 to set up

> Welsh-medium circulating charity schools aimed at teaching people of all ages to read the Bible and to learn the Church Catechism. This was the first major effort through the medium of Welsh to educate the common people of Wales, and it proved extremely successful. It is estimated that almost half the population of Wales during those years learned to read through his schools and, as a result, Wales in the middle years of the eighteenth century became one of the first countries in the modern world to become literate on any large scale.[6]

In that context, religious societies similar to the Methodist societies of England founded by John Wesley were started in Wales, and Daniel Rowlands and Howell Davies were the other prominent leaders of this movement. But in adopting Whitefield's Calvinism, the Welsh movement differed from the English revival movement which was Arminian in its theology.[7] Wesley emphasized human's

---

4 Paul Chambers, *Religion, Secularization and Social Change in Wales: Congregational Studies in a Post Christian Society*, (Cardiff: University of Wales Press, 2004), p. 4.

5 William Williams, *Welsh Calvinistic Methodism: A Historical Sketch*, (London. James Nisbet and Co., 1872), p. 7. Hereafter cited as Williams, *Welsh Calvinistic Methodism.*

6 E. Wyn James, "'The New Birth of a People': Welsh Language and Identity and the Welsh Methodists, *c.*1740–1820," in Pope, *Religion and National Identity,* p.24.

7 "United Kingdom and Ireland," in *Historical Dictionary of the Reformed Churches*, ed. by Robert Benedetto, Donald K. McKim, (Maryland: Scarecrow Press, Inc., 2010, 2nd ed.), pp. 494-5. Hereafter cited as *Historical Dictionary.* Williams says, "The great Calvinistic controversy began in 1770,...From this time there was a complete separation between Mr. Wesley and his people... and the Calvinistic Methodists." Williams, *Welsh Calvinistic Methodism,* pp. 139-40.

free will while Whitefield emphasized God's sovereignty in the salvation of human.

Initially, the Welsh Calvinistic Methodist movement developed within the Church of England. According to R. T. Jones, "there was no official Methodist 'denomination' in Wales in 1800, although the Calvinistic Methodists were rapidly growing apart from the Church of England." [8] And Geraint Tudur noted that "these religious groups…were in a unique position; though claiming to be Anglican in spirit, they were not governed by the hierarchy of the Church. They made their own rules and sometimes seemed perilously close to Dissenting."[9] Lay "exhorters" and ministerial and lay superintendents worked with the Welsh religious societies. The first Association of the Welsh Calvinistic Methodists, presided by George Whitefield, was held at Watford, Glamorganshire, on January 5 and 6, 1742. The purpose was "to devise means to bring the numerous converts which had been already made under some spiritual supervision and to concert measures for the further extension of the great work."[10]

After some period of decline marred by division, persecution and then recovery, Thomas Charles of Bala, an Anglican minister who had become a leader in the movement, ordained eight exhorters on the 20th of June 1811, and in August of the same year, "thirteen chosen from among those of the South, were ordained at an Association at Llandilo Fawr."[11] Henderson remarked that they "resorted to ordination" since "the Church of England proved unco-operative."[12] This action, along with increasing persecution, led to a break with the Church of England.

At this juncture, we must note the significance of the tie between Howell Harris and George Whitefield by extensively quoting David Ceri Jones who writes:

---

8 R. Tudur Jones, *Faith and the Crisis of a Nation: Wales 1890–1914*, ed. by Robert Pope, (Cardiff: University of Wales Press, 2004), p. 32.

9 Geraint Tudur, "'Thou Bold Champion," in Pope, *Religion and National Identity*, p. 47.

10 Williams, *Welsh Calvinistic Methodism*, p. 18.

11 Williams, *Welsh Calvinistic Methodism*, p. 193.

12 G. D. Henderson, *Presbyterianism*, (Aberdeen: The University Press, 1956), p. 147.

> Any study which attempts to understand how the Welsh revival related to the wider evangelical movement must focus, initially at least, on the activities of these two men....Through his friendship with Whitefield, Harris became an integral part of the London evangelical scene. During his many extended visits to the London Methodists he found himself at the hub of the international community as news and information about the revival from throughout the British Atlantic world flooded in....[Harris ensured] that his fellow Methodists back home were enabled to take advantage of every opportunity that the wider revival afforded them and that the progress of the Welsh revival was known throughout the international revival.[13]

Therefore, the Welsh Calvinistic Methodist Church was not initiated in isolation but was always an integral part of a larger evangelical movement. And as we shall see, they were also regarded as "Presbyterian" which engaged them with the wider ecumenical movement.

4.1.2. The Presbyterian Church of Wales: The Welsh Calvinistic Methodists organized their church into two synods, one for North Wales and one for South Wales. On the 11th of March 1823, the church drafted its own Confession of Faith based on the Westminster Confession, Rules of Discipline, and church polity.[14] That they begun to identify themselves as "Presbyterian" was depicted by Drysdale who observed:

> the organization became more and more distinctively Presbyterian; though it was not till [May] 1864, when the Calvinistic Methodism both of North and South Wales put itself under the control of one common 'General Assembly,' that the Presbyterianism of its government became more clearly manifest, and the Presbyterian name began to be used.[15]

---

13 David Ceri Jones, *A Glorious Work in the World: Welsh Methodism and the International Evangelical Revival, 1735–1750,* (Cardiff: University of Wales Press, 2004), pp. 9-10.

14 *Historical Dictionary*, p. 495.

15 A. H. Drysdale, *History of the Presbyterians in England*, (London: Publication Committee of the Presbyterian Church of England, 1889), p. 595.

Others also considered them as "Presbyterian" and this was evident from the *Report of Proceedings of the Second General Council of the Presbyterian Alliance*, which was convened at Philadelphia on September, 1880. This report states:

> To the Church of Howell Harris, of Griffith Jones, of Charles of Bala, and of a goodly host of other worthies; church baptized in the blood and fire of persecution; Methodist in name, Calvinistic in doctrine, Presbyterian in polity, of unblemished orthodoxy and apostolic zeal, right welcome art thou to a place in this Presbyterian Council.[16]

From these statements, we can asserts that the Welsh Calvinistic Methodist definitely identified themselves as Presbyterian, as do others, at least in the latter part of the 19th century (see fig. 2), particularly in reference to their ecclesiastical polity. But it was only in 1928 that they formally adopted "The Presbyterian Church of Wales" as their title.[17]

4.1.3. The Welsh Calvinistic Methodist Foreign Mission and the formation and development of the Presbyterian Church of India: The Welsh Calvinistic Methodists supported the London Missionary Society both in terms of home support and also in overseas agency till they resolved to establish a Foreign Missionary Society of their own in 1840. J. H. Morris says this is the outcome of difference in theology and church polity with other members of the London Missionary Society.[18] Soon after forming the Welsh Calvinistic Methodist Foreign Mission, the Rev. Thomas Jones was sent to Khasi Hills on 22nd June 1841. The baptism of the first converts on March 1846 "marked the beginning of a permanently established church in

---

16 *Report of Proceedings of the Second General Council of the Presbyterian Alliance*, ed. by John B. Dales and R. M. Patterson, (Philadelphia: Presbyterian Journal Company, 1880), p.43.

17 "Religion," *Wales Factfile*, (Cardiff: Institute of Welsh Affairs), http://www.clickonwales.org/wp-content/uploads/6_Factfile_Religion.pdf. (15 August 2013).

18 John H. Morris, *The History of the Welsh Calvinistic Methodists Foreign Mission: To the end of the Year 1904*, (Carnavon: The Calvinistic Methodists Bookroom, 1910), p. 25.

the Khasi-Jaintia Hills."[19] A Presbytery was formed in 1867 and in 1895 five Presbyteries were established that resulted in the formation of an Assembly of the Presbyteries in 1896.[20]

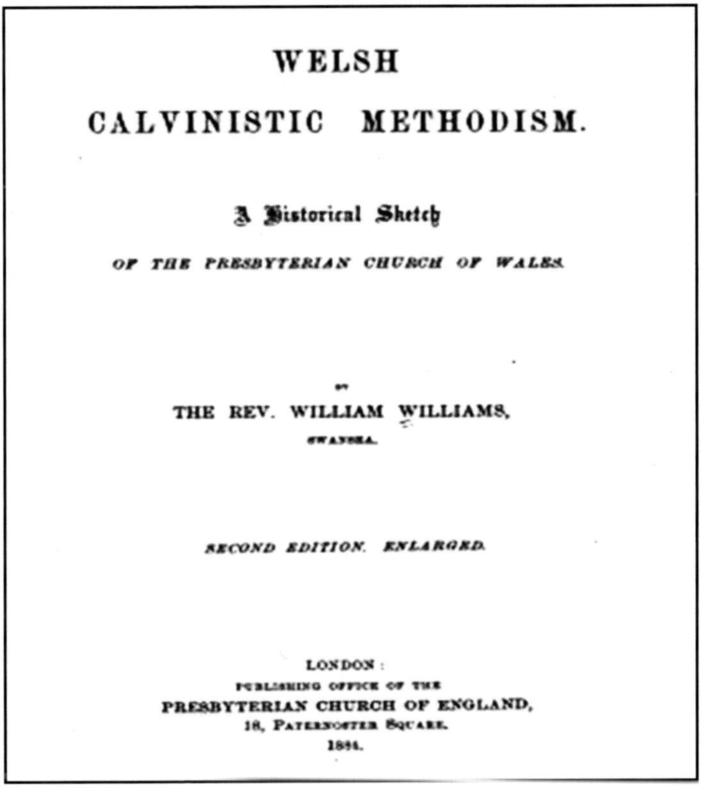

WELSH

CALVINISTIC METHODISM.

A Historical Sketch

OF THE PRESBYTERIAN CHURCH OF WALES.

THE REV. WILLIAM WILLIAMS,

SWANSEA.

SECOND EDITION. ENLARGED.

LONDON:

PUBLISHING OFFICE OF THE

PRESBYTERIAN CHURCH OF ENGLAND,

18, PATERNOSTER SQUARE.

1884.

Fig.2: The 2nd edition of William Williams' book published in 1884, titled *Welsh Calvinistic Methodism - A Historical Sketch of the Presbyterian Church of Wales.*

19 O. L. Snaitang, *Christianity and Social change in Northeast India*, (Shillong:Vendrame Institute, 1993), p. 72. We must note that the Serampore Mission was engaged in mission work in the Khasi Hills around 1813 till 1838.

20 *Assembly of the Presbyterian Church in North East India Golden Jubilee Souvenir: 1926-1976*, (Shillong: Central Ward, 1976), pp. 4-5. Hereafter cited as *Assembly...Souvenir.*

Around this time, work was also being carried out in the region of Sylhet-Cachar Plains, and soon expanded into the Lushai Hills and the Cachar Hills. In 1905-06, there was a great revival in the Khasi Hills which had a great impact on these adjoining churches. As church membership grew, the Assembly that met at Shillong in 1923 decided to divide itself into three families, namely the Khasi-Jaintia Assembly, the Lushai Assembly and the Plains' Assembly which constituted the Synod of the Presbyterian Church in Assam in 1926. As the church expanded in other part of North East India, the name was changed to the Assembly of the Presbyterian Church in North-East India in 1972, and eventually assumed the name Presbyterian Church of India (PCI) in 1992.[21]

At this point, we must note that there were various Presbyterian Foreign Missions that entered India in the 19th century who agreed to form the Presbyterian Alliance of India (hereafter referred to as PAI) in December 1875. From the "Minutes of the First Conference of Presbyterian Confederation," held on 5th January, 1871, those involved were the Church of Scotland, Free Church of Scotland, United Presbyterian Church of Scotland, English, Welsh and Irish Presbyterians, American Presbyterian Church, Reformed Church in America, United Presbyterian Church of North America and Dutch Reformed Presbyterian Church in Ceylon.[22] At the beginning of the 20th century, there were twelve Presbyterian and Reformed Churches in India. These different Presbyterian families formed a union in 1901 which was tentatively called "the Church of Christ in India (Presbyterian)" and they later became "the Presbyterian Church in India" on 19th December 1904.[23] But the Welsh Calvinistic Methodist Church, along with the United Presbyterian Church of North America, the Reformed Presbyterian Church of North America, the United Original Secession Church of Scotland, and the Bengal Evangelistic Mission of Gopalgunge "did not concur in

21 *Assembly...Souvenir*, pp. 6, 8, 25; *Constitution of the Presbyterian,* pp. ii.

22 As quoted by K. L. Parker, The Development of the United Church of Northern India, (A Dissertation submitted to the Faculty of the Divinity School in Candidacy for the Degree of Doctor of Philosophy, Chicago, Illinois, 1935), pp. 36, 43. Hereafter cited as Parker, The Development.

23 Parker, The Development, pp. 84, 97.

the union."[24] The Presbyterian Church in India later merged with Congregationalists in south and north India to form the South India United Church and the United Church of North India in 1908 and 1924 respectively.

4.2 Factors Influencing the Formulation of the Confession of Faith of the Presbyterian Church of India

During the drafting of "Statement of Doctrine and Questions for the Ordaining of Office-Bearers in the Native Churches of India" by the PAI, the Welsh Calvinist missionaries expressed their satisfaction to adopt the Westminster Confession as a doctrinal statement. Others who favoured this Confession too also argued

> that it is a strong, well-tried mould into which to pour the young Church of India; that this young unformed body needs just a clear, full strong statement of doctrine at this period of its growth; that the time for Creed-making in India has not yet come, and it is a mistake to 'waste our time, and energies in amateur creed-making when we are already united in creed.'[25]

Those who were not in favour proposed following the Presbyterians of Japan who were united on the "Apostles Creed," complemented by short statements about the Holy Spirit, the Scriptures and the Divinity of Christ (see fig. 3) and argued that

> the plastic state of the India Church is the very best time to put on it the stamp not so much of the languages of the Westminster theologians as of the Apostles; that it is well to have a brief, irenic, creed which has in view not only the union of all Presbyterians in India, but looks forward to a larger union.[26]

Finally, it was resolved by the committee on completing the Basis of Union that "the 'Confession of Faith of the South India United Church (SIUC), as now modified, be recommended for

---

24 Parker, *The Development*, p. 98.

25 Parker, *The Development*, p. 86.

26 Parker, *The Development*, p. 87.

adoption as the Confession of Faith of the United Church In India.'" This SIUC Confession was further an adaptation of *Short Statement of the Three Scotch Mission*.[27] The SIUC Confession of Faith was adopted by the Presbyterian Church in India in its first General Assembly in 1904.[28] A Preamble settled the conflicting views on the significance of the Westminster Confession and other Confessions (see fig.4). Comparing the SIUC Confession of Faith with the modified Confession, Parker write

> the latter is better worded and better divided. It has introduced some phrases from the Westminster Shorter Catechism,… and inserted a clear statement of the doctrine of election. The earlier Confession was more suitable for the union to which the Southern Synod was already looking forward.[29]

When South India Synod became part of the South India United Church in 1907,[30] the Confession of Faith was retained by the Presbyterian Church in India, who further adopted it when they merged with the Congregational Churches of Western India on the 30th December 1924 to become the United Church of North India (UCNI).[31]

---

27 Parker, *The Development,* p. 86. Here "South India United Church" refers to the union of the American Arcot Mission and the United Free Church of Scotland Mission. Bengt Sundkler, *Church of South India: The Movement Towards Union, 1900-1947*, (London: Lutterworth Press, 1954), pp. 36-7.

28 *Minutes of the First General Assembly of the Presbyterian Church in India*, Allahabad, December, 19, 1904. (Cyclostyled).

29 Parker, *The Development,* p. 87.

30 *Minutes of the Fourth General Assembly of the Presbyterian Church in India*, Calcutta, December, 31, 1907. (Cyclostyled). This was the consummation of the resolution made by the Provisional General Assembly of the Presbyterian Church in India that "the request of the South India Synod to continue negotiations looking to a wider union be granted." *Minutes of the First General Assembly of the Presbyterian Church in India*, Allahabad, December, 19, 1904. (Cyclostyled). See also Edwin J. Palmer, "Towards Unity," in *The Christian Task in India*, ed. by John McKenzie, (London: MacMillan and Co., Ltd, 1929), pp. 267, 272. Hereafter cited as Palmer, "Towards Unity."

31 *Minutes of the First General Assembly of the United Church of India* (North), Bombay, December, 30, 1924. (Cyclostyled).

CONFESSION OF FAITH AND CONSTITUTION OF THE CHURCH OF CHRIST IN JAPAN

CONFESSION OF FAITH

The Lord Jesus Christ, whom we worship as God, the only begotten Son of God, for us men and for our salvation was made man and suffered. He offered up a perfect sacrifice for sin; and all who are one with Him by faith are pardoned and accounted righteous; and faith in Him working by love purifies the heart.

The Holy Ghost, who with the Father and the Son is worshipped and glorified, reveals Jesus Christ to the soul; and without His grace man being dead in sin cannot enter the kingdom of God. By Him the prophets and apostles and holy men of old were inspired; and He speaking in the Scriptures of the Old and the New Testaments is the supreme and infallible judge in all things pertaining unto faith and living.

From these Holy Scriptures the ancient Church of Christ drew its confession; and we holding the faith once delivered to the saints, join in that confession with praise and thanksgiving:—

I believe in God the Father Almighty, Maker of Heaven and Earth.

And in Jesus Christ His only Son our Lord; who was conceived by the Holy Ghost, born of the Virgin Mary; suffered under Pontius Pilate, was crucified, dead and buried, He descended into Hades; the third day He rose from the dead; He ascended into Heaven, and sitteth at the right hand of God the Father Almighty; from thence He shall come to judge the quick and the dead.

I believe in the Holy Ghost; the Holy Catholic Church; the communion of saints; the forgiveness of sins; the resurrection of the body, and the life everlasting. AMEN.

Fig. 3: "Confession of Faith of the Church of Christ in Japan," reproduced from *Report of Commission II: The Church in the Mission Field.* Edinburgh: WMC, 1910, p. 294.

Preamble

The Presbyterian Church in India adopting the following as its Confession of Faith, to be subscribed by ministers, licentiates, and elders, does not thereby reject any of the doctrine standards of the parent Churches, but, on the contrary, commends them—especially the Westminster Confession of Faith, the Welsh Calvinistic Confession of Faith, and the Confession and Canons of the Synod of Dort—as worthy exponents of the Word of God, and as systems of doctrine to be taught in our churches and seminaries.

Article I

The Scriptures of the Old and New Testaments are the Word of God, and the only infallible rule of faith and duty.

Fig. 4: Portion of "Confession of Faith of the Presbyterian Church in India," reproduced from *Report of Commission II: The Church in the Mission Field.* Edinburgh: WMC, 1910, p. 297.

Although the Welsh Calvinistic Methodist in India did not become a part of the Presbyterian Church in India in 1904,[32] the efforts to bring into the union other Churches in North India following the Presbyterian system continued. Because of this, "a delegate from the Welsh Calvinistic Methodist Church of Assam" attended the General Assembly of Presbyterian Church in India at Nagpur in December 1917.[33] This Assembly resolved to "send three delegates to the Assam Assembly of the Welsh Calvinistic Methodist Church in the ensuing years."[34] In its next meeting at Calcutta in 1919, the Assembly welcomed the Welsh Church to its membership, making a special concession, in view of the peculiar circumstances, which left the Assam Church free to continue its own rules as far as it might wish, and fixed a definite rate for its assessment and representation in the General Assembly.[35] Thus, they eventually became a member in 1919. So, their participations in the union process and their association with other Presbyterian families had surely influenced the formulation of the Confession of Faith that was adopted by the Presbyterian Church in Assam (later the PCI) in 1924.

4.3 Confession of Faith of the PCI and the Question of Originality

At this point, an important question that needs to be raised is to what extent this influence bears its marks upon the PCI Confession

32 Parker says that delegates were sent only twice in the meetings of the union committee, partly due to the remote location of the mission field, although they shown their interest by sending suggestions for changes in the drafted document for the union. He quoted the *Indian Standard* for Oct. 1905 which suggested that the Welsh mission received a large amount of money "with the condition attached that if the name of the Church was changed the money would be forfeited." Parker, *The Development*, p. 103.

33 Palmer, "Towards Unity," p. 272.

34 *Minutes of the Ninth General Assembly of the Presbyterian Church in India*, Nagpur, December, 28, 1917. (Cyclostyled).

35 Palmer, "Towards Unity," pp. 272-3. The General Assembly authorized the representatives of the negotiating parties to consider "any differences in practice and procedure with a view to their adjustment" to consummate the union. *Minutes of the Tenth General Assembly of the Presbyterian Church in India*, Calcutta, December, 30, 1919. (Cyclostyled).

of Faith and how much does it bear the effort and creativity of the Welsh missionaries. There is a general consensus based upon Rosiamliana's assumption that the Welsh missionaries "received a copy of the draft constitution" of the UCNI and "copied down the draft of the Confession of Faith" and adopted it with a slight modification.[36] But this assumption can make the PCI Confession look excessively derivative and even its genuineness questionable.

In the previous section, it was mentioned that during the time of the Presbyterian Alliance of India, the Welsh missionaries had participated in the drafting process of a "Statement of Doctrine" with their input. Their influence upon the Confession of the Presbyterian Church in India was apparent from the endorsement of the Welsh Confession in the Preamble (see fig. 4) even though they did not assent in the Presbyterian union in 1904. So, we can argue that the Confession of Faith of the UCNI was essentially the outcome of their contribution and that the UCNI was effectively the beneficiary even if the Welsh missionaries may actually "copied" it later.

It was also likely that they were keen upon, and were familiar with, the outcome of the drafted "Statement of Doctrine" because the resulting Confession of Faith, as adopted by the Presbyterian Church in India from the SIUC, was so popular that even churches outside India adopted it much before the UNCI did.[37] Assuming that they were inspired by their previous effort, the Welsh missionaries perhaps drafted another one in line with that Confession of Faith which they

36 Rosiamliana Tochhawng, *A Study of the Ten Articles of Faith of the Presbyterian Church in India*, (Delhi: ISPCK, 2007), pp. 20-22. Hereafter cited as Rosiamliana, *Study of the Ten Articles*. Cf. H. Vanlalauva, *Hun Hnuhnung Thu: Mizoram Presbyterian Kohhran 2011 Nilai leh Beihrual Thupui*, (Aizawl: SL&PB, 2010), pp. 184-5. Hereafter cited as Vanlalauva, *Hun Hnuhnung Thu*; R. Lalthanmawia, *Reinterpretation of Calvin in the Light of the Ten Articles of Faith of the Presbyterian Church of India*, (Unpublished material). Hereafter cited as Lalthanmawia, *Reinterpretation of Calvin*. C. Lalsangliana, *Kohhran Thurin*, (Aizawl: SL&PB, 2014), p. 24.

37 L. George Paik, *The History of Protestant Missions in Korea, 1832-1910*, (Pyongyang: Union Christian College Press, 1927), p. 389. Jae-Buhm Hwang even calls it "the first Asian ecumenical confession of faith." Jae-Buhm Hwang, "The first Asian Ecumenical Confession of Faith: The So-Called Twelve Articles of Faith of Many Asian Protestant Churches," *The Ecumenical Review*, Vol. 63/2, July 2011, p. 200.

partly prepared. And since they had a firsthand knowledge of, and critically engaged with, that Confession right from its "drafting process", they must have the confidence to even alter it when they felt the need to do so.

In this regard, it is noteworthy that among those who adopted that Confession, including the UCNI, only the Presbyterian Church of Assam actually seemed to be seriously engaged with the formulation and even added their "touch" by narrowing it down to Ten Articles from the original Twelve. In that process, their most significant "touch" must be the exclusion of "the doctrine of election" from Article IX which state:

> While God chose a people in Christ before the foundation of the world, that they should be holy and without blemish before Him in love; having foreordained them unto adoption as sons (sic) through Jesus Christ unto Himself, according to the good pleasure of His will....[38]

Seeing the keenness the Mizo Christians shown to the doctrines of election and predestination (see Chap. 3.3.3), it can be a deliberate "choice" on the part of the missionaries to exclude this important "tenet" while they previously expressed their satisfaction with the Westminster Confession (see section 4.2) where the theme of election is so prominent.[39] Moreover, we must also consider the fact that D. E. Jones, the Welsh missionary, translated the Welsh Confession of Faith into Mizo which was used as a Confessional statement until 1924.[40] In the Welsh Confession, "the election of grace" was a recurring theme,[41] hence, omitting it must be deliberate.

Another alteration they made was the wording in Article X itself where the word, "receive" was changed into "judged". As a

38 "Confession of Faith and Constitution of the Presbyterian Church in India," in *Report of Commission II: The Church in the Mission Field*. Edinburgh: World Missionary Conference, 1910, p. 298.

39 See *Westminster Confession,* Chap. 3; 8:5, 8; 35:2.

40 Vanlalthlana, *Doctrine of Grace: Augustine's Doctrine of Grace and Human Free Will and an Appraisal from a Mizo Christian Perspective*, (Delhi: ISPCK, 2010), p. 282.

41 See *Welsh Confession*, Chap. 12,14, 20, 33, 34.

result, the tone was changed from "shall receive according to the deeds done in this present life whether good or bad" into "shall be judged according to the deeds done in this present life whether good or bad." We shall see its implications later in chapter 5. Article X also had a "happy ending" as it culminated with the lot of the believers while the Confession of the Presbyterian Church in India closed with the destiny of the "condemned".

Considering these factors, it was doubtful that they simply altered the draft of the UCNI just for the sake of alteration. It was most likely that they considered the North East Christian mindset along with the background context of the drafting process and the original formulae on which the draft was based. So, instead of opting for the Westminster Confession of Faith or the Welsh Confession, they ultimately decided to frame one in line with the Confession of Faith of the Presbyterian Church in India.[42]

If this be the case, we need to move beyond the Presbyterian Church in India or UCNI's Confession of Faith and go back to the plausible "formulae" on which the Presbyterian Alliance in India originally depended. Through comparison, we can see that the Confession of Faith of the Presbyterian Church in India closely resembled some of the wordings of the Longer and Shorter Westminster Catechisms.[43] It has been mentioned that they "introduced some phrases from the Westminster Shorter Catechism" when they adopted the *Confession* of the SIUC. So, the Westminster Catechisms is one of it sources.

Earlier, it has been stated that the *Confession* of the SIUC was an adaptation of *Short Statement of the Three Scotch Mission*. The Scottish influence was also obvious from the Preamble of this *Confession* where "the doctrinal standards of the parent churches of Scotland and America" along with "the Westminster and Heidelberg

42 *The Constitution of the Presbyterian Church in Assam*, (Aijal: The Welsh Mission Bookroom, 1925), pp. vi-vii,1.

43 Meant to be a summary of the Westminster Confession, Dr. Anthony Tuckney was credited as writing the more comprehensive Larger Catechism while the simpler Shorter Catechism was credited to Rev. John Wallis. *The Constitution of the Presbyterian Church, (USA): Part I - Book of Confessions*, (Louisville: The Office of the General Assembly, 1996), p. 124. Hereafter cited as *Book of Confessions.*

catechisms" and "the Westminster Confession" was endorsed.[44] And though we cannot retrieve the *Short Statement*, it is probably derived from, or even similar to the *Summary of Principles* (see fig. 5) which was meant to be a summary of the Westminster Confession in the United Presbyterian Church of Scotland, one of the three Scottish Missions that actively participated in the PAI as well as the SIUC. What we can infer is that the *Confession* of the SIUC and the Presbyterian Church in India was actually a concise amalgamation of the Westminster Catechisms and the *Summary of Principles.* This agrees with Curtis' account that unions of the Presbyterian Mission Churches in India have been attained on "the bases of eleven and of twelve short Articles epitomizing the doctrine of the Westminster Confession along similar lines, positive, Scriptural, and noncontroversial, emphasizing the particular doctrines most required by missionary circumstances.[45]

Thus, the Confession of the Presbyterian Church in Assam need not be a "copy" of the draft of the UCNI. While their participations in the union process and their association with other Presbyterian families had surely influenced the formulation of the *Confession,* the Welsh missionaries may be considering the context of the North East people and probably wanted to leave their "creative" mark too. Therefore, looking at the original sources from which the Presbyterian Church in India's *Confession* was adopted, they could have made an arrangement and so drafted the Ten Articles of Faith.[46]

---

44 Parker, *The Development,* pp. 86, 187.

45 William A. Curtis, *A History of Creeds and Confessions of Faith in Christendom and Beyond*, (Aberdeen: Aberdeen University, 1911), pp. 283-4. Hereafter cited as Curtis, *History of Creeds.*

46 This view acknowledges the unique identity and originality that the Presbyterian Church in Assam had from the UCNI (later the CNI), especially in terms of their geographical location as well as their missionaries. Jyrwa notes that when the Khasi Church considered the geographical distance of the area and "the problem that the churches in North East face which others might not really appreciate," they did not favour to become a part of the CNI. And the rest of the North East Presbyterian churches were likely to share their conviction that "developments in terms of Church union would be first in a limited area of North East." J. Fortiswell Jyrwa, *A Historical Study on the Growth and*

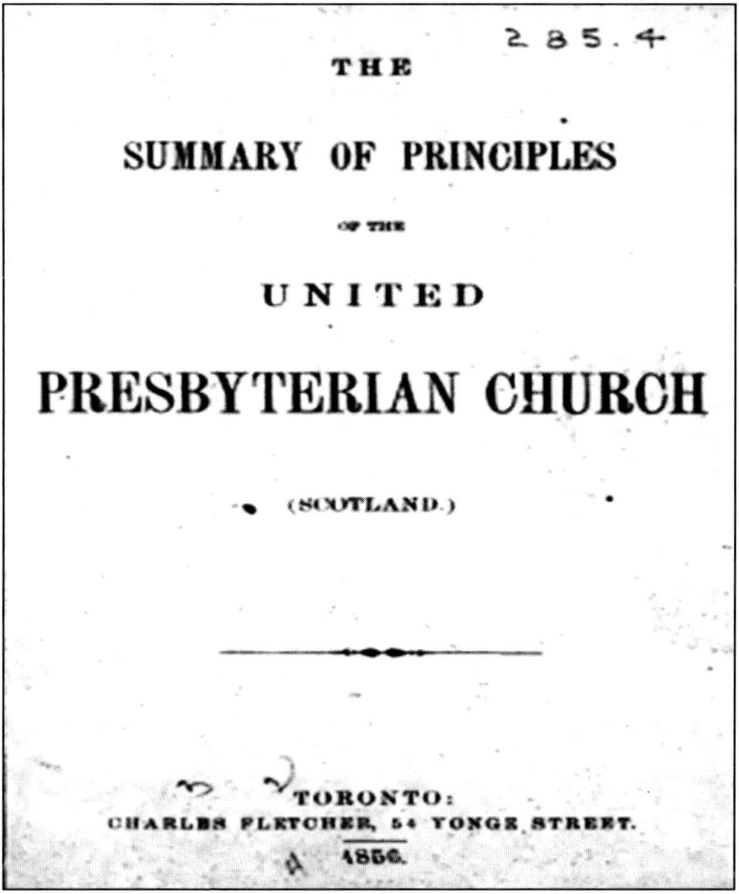

THE

SUMMARY OF PRINCIPLES

OF THE

UNITED

PRESBYTERIAN CHURCH

(SCOTLAND.)

TORONTO:
CHARLES FLETCHER, 54 YONGE STREET.
1856.

Fig. 5: The cover of *Summary of Principles* that was meant "to promote the end in view, namely, that of affording, especially to persons seeking admission into the fellowship of the Church, a distinct account of the rise and past history of the Church, and of the views of divine truth which it holds." *Summary of Principles of the United Presbyterian Church (Scotland)*, (Toronto: Charles Fletcher, 1856), p. 1.

Development of the Khasi-Jaintia Presbyterian Church in the Twentieth Century, (MTh Thesis submitted to the Senate of Serampore, 1974), pp. 120-1.

4.4 Main Theme/Motif of Article X of the PCI Confession of Faith

4.4.1. Overview of the PCI Confession of Faith: Looking at these earlier formulations on which the PCI *Confession* was based, we can say they were actually drawn from Calvin's *Institutes of the Christian Religion.* It also agreed with Curtis' remark that the Westminster Confession of Faith "was the last great Creed-utterance of Calvinism, and intellectually and theologically it is a worthy child of the *Institutes*, a stately and noble standard for Bible-loving [person]."[47] Thus, Calvin's *Institutes* was fundamental to the PCI Confession of Faith and must be seen in the light of it.

From this perspective, we can see that some distinct tenets of Calvinism were left out for the sake of brevity and ecumenicity. The PCI *Confession* does not specifically refer to *unconditional election* and *limited atonement* for which the Westminster Confession was criticized and seen as lacking a "philosophical foundation for mission."[48] The Articles of the PCI *Confession* were condensed from these "sources" and arranged subject wise. This arrangement compartmentalized what was a system of doctrine into a self-contained unit. Particularly, what was previously a statement on "the application of salvation" now becomes a statement about the Last Day in Article X of the PCI Confession of Faith.

4.4.2. Main theme/motif of Article X of the PCI Confession of Faith: Article X of the PCI Confession of Faith is basically understood as an eschatological doctrine.[49] To determine its main motif, we need to compare it with the 'eschatological content' of other creedal confessions - the Apostle's Creed, the Nicene Creed, the Westminster

---

47 Curtis, *History of Creeds,* p. 275.

48 Kenneth Cracknell, *Justice, Courtesy and Love: Theologians and Missionaries Encountering the World Religions*, 1846-1914 (London: Epworth Press, 1995), p.22; see *Westminster Confession,* Chap. 3; 8:5, 8; 35:2.

49 Saiaithanga, *Thurin Zirna*, 5th rev. ed. (Aizawl: SPB, 1989), p.66; Rosiamliana, *Study of the Ten Articles,* pp. 55, 87-90; Chuauthuama, "Mizo Kristiante Hun Hnuhnung Thlir Dan," in *Calvina Zirtirna leh Mizo Nun*, ed. by Vanlalchhuanawma, (Aizawl: Calvin Study Center, 2000), p. 59. Hereafter cited as Chuauthuama, "Hun Hnuhnung Thlir Dan."

Confession of Faith and the Welsh Confession of Faith - which the preamble of the Confession of Faith of the PCI commended as "worthy exposition of the Word of God, and as systems of doctrine to be taught in its Churches and seminaries."[50]

The eschatological content of the Apostle's Creed is that Jesus "shall come to judge the quick and the dead" with an affirmation of belief in "the resurrection of the body, and life everlasting."[51] This is quite similar with the Nicene's Creed affirmation that Jesus "shall come again with glory to judge both the quick and the dead" and that "we look for the resurrection of the dead, and the life of the world to come."[52] In both of these, the second coming of Jesus Christ to judge everyone was very prominent. Another focus was upon the bodily resurrection of believers to have an everlasting life.

The Westminster Confession has 33 chapters and the last two deals with the "last things." Chapter 32, titled "Of the State of Men (sic) after Death, and of the Resurrection of the Dead" basically focuses on the immediate state of the soul upon death, and the nature of the living and the dead body of human being in the Last Day. Chapter 33, titled "Of the Last Judgment" basically focuses on the day when Jesus Christ will judge the world in righteousness, and everyone will receive according to what he/she had done in the body. This day will manifest the glory of God's mercy and justice.[53]

---

50 *Constitution of the Presbyterian,* p. 1. Prior to the amendment of the PCI Constitution in 2004, "the Apostles Creed, Nicene Creed, Westminster Confession of Faith and the Confession of Faith of the Presbyterian Church of Wales" were not explicitly mentioned but categorically put as "the doctrinal standards of the parent Churches" in the preamble of the *Constitution.* Cf. *The Constitution of the Presbyterian Church in Assam,* (Aijal: The Welsh Mission Bookroom, 1925), p. 1; *The Constitution of the Presbyterian Church in Assam,* (Aijal: The Loch Printing Press, 1955), p. 1; *The Constitution of the Presbyterian Church in NE India,* (Shillong: The Khasi Jaintia Presbyterian Press, 1968), p. 1; *The Constitution of the Presbyterian Church of India,* (Shillong: The Khasi Jaintia Synod Press, 1993), p. 1.

51 *Book of Confessions,* p. 7.

52 *Book of Confessions,* p. 3.

53 *Book of Confessions,* pp. 163-4.

The Welsh Confession of Faith "is in every important feature in unison with the Westminster Confession of Faith and the Articles of the Church of England."[54] According to Curtis, it was basically "a statement of the Westminster doctrine."[55] Having forty four articles, the last four chapters can be considered as eschatological. Chapter 41, titled "Of Death, and the State of Men (sic) after Death" basically focused on the immediate state of the soul upon death; chapter 42, titled "Of the Resurrection" deals with the resurrection of the whole humankind; chapter 43, titled "Of the General Judgment" professes that everyone will stand before the judgment of Jesus Christ; and chapter 44, titled "Of the Eternal State of the Righteous and Unrighteous" professes that human's eternal destiny will be determined by the judgment of Jesus Christ.[56]

Although the Shorter Catechism and the Summary of Principles are not mentioned directly in the preamble of the PCI *Confession*, Article XII of the Presbyterian Church in India's Confession and Article X of the Confession of the Presbyterian Church in Assam closely resemble it. The relevant portions, in line with the sequence above, states:

> At the resurrection, believers, being raised up in glory, shall be openly acknowledged and acquitted in the Day of Judgment, and made perfectly blessed in the full enjoying of God to all eternity.[57]

> At death the souls of believers are made perfect in holiness, and depart to be with Christ. Their blessedness shall be completed at the last day, when their souls shall be reunited to their bodies then raised incorruptible; and after being in the general Judgment acquitted, and acknowledged as the saved

54 Williams, *Welsh Calvinistic Methodism*, p. 205.

55 Curtis, *History of Creeds*, p. 286.

56 *Manual of Worship of the Presbyterian Church of India*, (Shillong: The Presbyterian Church of India, 2002), pp.109-114. Hereafter cited as *Manual of Worship of the PCI.*

57 *Book of Confessions,* p. 184.

> of the Lord, they shall be taken to heaven, where they shall be perfectly "blessed in the full enjoying of God to all eternity."[58]
>
> At the last day the dead shall be raised, and all shall appear before the judgment seat of Christ, and shall receive according to the deeds done in this present life whether good or bad. Those who have believed in Christ and obeyed Him shall be openly acquitted and received into glory; but the unbelieving and wicked, being condemned, shall suffer the punishment due to their sins.[59]
>
> At the last day the dead shall be raised and all shall appear before the judgment seat of Christ and shall be judged according to the deeds done in this present life whether good or bad. The unbelieving and wicked, being condemned, shall suffer the punishment due to their sins, but those who have believed in Christ and obeyed Him shall be openly acquitted and received into glory.[60]

These four statements closely resemble chapters 32 and 33 of the Westminster Confession of Faith which is universally considered authoritative for the Reformed Churches.[61] But, while the Westminster Confession guided the formulation of the Confession of the Presbyterian Church in India, and consequently the PCI, certain "orthodox" tenets were left out and only the bare minimum necessary was retained keeping in mind the young Indian churches

---

58 *Summary of Principles of the United Presbyterian Church (Scotland)*, (Toronto: Charles Fletcher, 1856), p. 9.

59 *Minutes of the First General Assembly of the Presbyterian Church in India*, Allahabad, December, 19, 1904. (Cyclostyled).

60 *Manual of Worship of the PCI.*, p. 117.

61 MacPherson argued that the Westminster Confession is "the most correct and balanced" in its representation of genuine Calvinism of all the Reformed formularies. John MacPherson, *The Westminster Confession of Faith with Introduction and Notes*, (Edinburg: T&T Clark,1881), p. 21. Hereafter cited as MacPherson, *Westminster Confession.* Curtis even state of its significance thus, "The English-speaking Presbyterian Churches throughout the world without exception adhere either to it or to some comparatively slight modification of it." Curtis, *History of Creeds*, p. 276.

and the emerging ecumenical spirit of the time.[62] In this regard, Palmer observed:

> They omit certain truths...which, presumably, did not command at the time of the union such universal consent. In the face of history it is impossible to affirm that because the Church or a Church omits from its creed or confession a certain truth, it may be assumed not to believe it.[63]

Hence, the main theme of Article X is the general resurrection and the final judgment of the living and the dead by Christ in the Last Day. The key word, which is the tenet for judgment, is good and bad deeds "done in this present life", basing on which believers will be received unto glory, and unbelievers and sinners punished for their sins. We shall look at the implications of this "key word" later.

4.4.3. Biblical and Theological basis of the Article X with special reference to "shall be judge according to the deeds done in this present life whether good or bad": What we can determine so far is that Article X was not a contextual formulation but an adaptation of Western eschatology which was, nonetheless, meant to suit the young churches of North East India. While this affirmation depicts its historical rootedness, an important question is whether there is a biblical and theological basis for the Article X and how to ascertain this?

Although the Confession of Faith adopted by the Presbyterian Church in Assam does not have any scriptural reference as such, the Westminster Confession from which it was primarily drawn upon,

---

62 We have mentioned that some participants in the drafting committee proposed to have "a brief, irenic, creed which has in view not only the union of all Presbyterians in India, but look forward to a larger union." Parker, *The Development*, p. 87.

63 Palmer, *The Christian Task*, p. 279. Notable omission included the immediate state of the soul after dead which asserted three orthodox doctrinal position: i) the soul as active in the immediate presence of Christ, and not as soul-sleep; ii) the soul as immediately in a state of rewards and punishments; iii) no intermediate condition, opposing the idea of purgatory, which countered the Roman Catholic believe of purgatory. MacPherson, *Westminster Confession*, p. 165.

"comes with a proof from the scripture"[64] to support the Articles. According to MacPherson, the Westminster Confession was received as "a statement of the truth contained in Scripture, and not as a document in itself authoritative apart from its scriptural ground" by the church members.[65] Thus, the claim of scriptural proof presupposed the acceptance of the Bible in a literal or metaphorical sense so that each paragraph of the Confession would be the accurate teaching of Scriptural truth, brought together in a comprehensive way. Whether one agrees that these scriptural passages support the claim of the Confession or not was more a matter of theological orientation.

From the biblical passages given in the Westminster Confession on eschatology that corresponded with Article X, the following passages particularly refers to "judgment according to the deeds done in this present life whether good or bad":

i. 2 Cor 5:10, Eccl 12:14, Rom 2:16; 14:10,12, Matt 12:36, 37 for the basis of the judgment, that is, according to one's deeds;

ii. Rom 2:5-6, 2 Thess 1:7-8, Rom 9:22, Matt 25:41, 46, 2 Thess 1:9, Isa 66:24, Mark 9:47-48 for the verdict given to the wicked and the unbelievers, that is, the punishment for their sin;

iii. Matt 25.31-34, Acts 3.19, 2 Thess 1.7, Ps 16.11 for the verdict given to the believers who are obedient, that is, an open acquittal and being received into glory. [66]

The Westminster Confession of Faith also contains theological basis or validations for the Day of Judgment that comes with scriptural support:

---

64 *The Westminster Confession of Faith and Catechisms in Modern English*, 3rd ed., (Michigan: Evangelical Presbyterian Church, 2010), pp. 52-3. Hereafter cited as *The Westminster...in Modern English.*

65 MacPherson, *Westminster Confession*, p.1.

66 Other passages were: i. Job 19:26-27, 2 Cor 15:42-44 for the resurrection of the dead; ii. Acts 17:31 for the Day of Judgment which God appointed; iii. John 5:27 for Jesus Christ as the judge in the Last Judgment; iv. 1 Cor 6:3, Jude 6, 2 Pet 2:4 and 2 Cor 5:10, Eccl 12:14, Rom 2:16; 14:10,12, Matt 12: 36,37 for the universality of the judgment which will include the apostate angels, believers and sinners.

> God's purpose in arranging for this day is to show forth the glory of his mercy in the eternal salvation of the elect and the glory of his justice in the damnation of the reprobates, who are wicked and disobedient.[67]
>
> Christ wants us to be completely convinced that there is going to be a day of judgment, as a deterrent to sin for everyone and as an added consolation for the godly in their suffering. He has also made sure that no one knows when that day will be, so that we may never rest secure in our worldly surroundings, but, not knowing what hour the Lord will come, we must always be alert and may always be ready to say, "Come, Lord Jesus, come quickly."[68]

Hence, we can say that the concept of "judgment according to one's deeds" in the Last Day has a theological validation from the scripture.

4.5 Justification Now – Resurrection and Judgment Later? An Important Existential Question

In the last section, we have mentioned that stressing "the deeds done in this present life" is a "key word". This clause negates the Roman Catholic Church's doctrine of purgatory and the church's power to shorten, lighten and even stop the sufferings of purgatory. In Roman Catholic teaching, "Purgatory" is a place of purification where the souls of believers who were not perfectly pure to enter heaven must undergo a process of cleansing and suffer to a varying degree and length. The duration and intensity of their suffering can be shortened and alleviated by the prayers and good works of the believers on earth, and especially by the sacrifice of the mass. It was related to the doctrine of "indulgences" which means the reduction by the Church of the temporal penalty incurred by sins that have already been forgiven - a transfer of credit from the pool of goodness to those

---

67 Scriptural references were Rom 9:23, Matt 25:21, Eph 2:4-7 and Rom 2:5-6, 2 Thess 1:7-8, Rom 9:22.

68 The scriptural bases given were 2 Pet 3:11,14, 2 Cor 5:10-11, 2 Thess 1:5-7, Luke 21:27-28, Rom 8:23-25 and Matt 24:36, 42-44, Mark 13:35-37, Luke 12:35-36, Rev 22:20.

whose accounts are in arrears. This doctrine gained significance when Pope Sixtus IV, in 1459, ruled that indulgences could commute not only the penance required on earth but also sufferings endured in Purgatory.[69]

But in the Mizo Christian context, stressing "the deeds done in this present life" leads to the problems that we have outlined in chapter three: How can we align it with the concept of "justification by faith"?[70] Moreover, does the final resurrection and judgment make sense when we hold that believers who were justified by faith through grace have a 'direct access' to heaven upon death? This existing tension between the teachings that "the soul of the dead immediately returns to God" and that "the resurrection and final judgment awaits" was evident from the questions send to *Kristian Tlangau* monthly magazine, the church's organ of the Mizoram Presbyterian Church. One church's elder asked the reliability of the teaching that the soul of the dead immediately returns to God over the Seventh Day Adventist's teaching on soul-sleep. Though the Church's teaching was affirmed in almost every funeral services, questions similar to this were raised from time to time in this magazine. Another church's elder even asked whether there was a lack of consistency in Presbyterian practice as it was affirmed that the soul of the dead immediately returns to God in the funeral service at home while the body was laid to rest at the tomb with the affirmation that it awaits the resurrection and final judgment in the second coming of Christ.[71] We shall attempt to address these questions by highlighting the concept of "justification by faith through grace" as expounded by Martin Luther and John Calvin. We shall see whether Luther and Calvin hold faith as negating good works. We shall also look at how

69 See "Indulgences," in *Encyclopedia of the Renaissance and the Reformation,* ed. by Jennifer Speake, et al., (New York: Facts On File, Inc, 2004), p. 252; Roland H. Bainton, *Here I Stand: A Life of Martin Luther*, (Tennessee: Abingdon Press, 1950), pp. 46-7. Hereafter cited as Bainton, *Here I Stand.*

70 In chapter 3.3.3, we have noted that those who stressed "justification by faith" have a tendency to downplay Christian duty as they overstressed faith and considered themselves as "beyond condemnation."

71 See *Kristian Tlangau Centenary Project: Kum 1911-2011 chhung atanga Editorial leh Zawhna leh Chhanna Lawrkhawm*,(Aizawl: SL&PB, 2011), pp. 365, 376, 378, 383, 386, 570.

Calvin understood "rewards" in the final judgment basing on one's deeds done in this life.

4.5.1. Martin Luther's understanding of "Justification by faith": Luther's understanding of "justification by faith" was the outcome of his struggle with the question of the righteousness of God. The prevailing understanding was largely influenced by Augustine and Scholasticism. For Augustine, a human being can attain salvation only by the grace of God alone and not through human merits. Thus, a human being absolutely depends upon the grace of God and God is the efficient cause of salvation.[72] Although medieval scholasticism[73] drew a lot from the ideas of Augustine as part of their common inheritance, it was Aristotle (384-322 B.C.) who was regarded as authoritative after the thirteenth century. So, the scholastic "doctrine of justification" leaned heavily on Aristotelian ethical ideas of "distributive justice" where righteousness meant "giving someone what they were entitled to."[74] This implied that justification took place on the basis of entitlement or merit, rather than grace. It created an "anxious conscience terrified by the inability to do enough to earn or merit salvation,"[75] as was evident from Luther's account of himself early in his life:

> I took [the justice of God] to mean that justice whereby God is just and deals justly in punishing the unjust. My situation was that...I stood before God troubled in conscience, and I had no confidence that my merit would assuage him.[76]

72 McGrath, *Christian Theology*, pp. 19, 367.

73 Scholasticism stressed "the rational justification of religious belief and the systematic presentation of those beliefs." McGrath, *Christian Theology*, p. 29. According to Harvey, scholasticism regards some authority to be binding and "is devoted to the detailed and often artificially elaborate refinement and extension of it." Van A. Harvey, "Scholasticism," in *A Handbook of Theological Terms*, (London: George Allen and Unwin Ltd., 1964), 186.

74 McGrath, *Christian Theology*, pp. 38-9.

75 H. J. Anderson, T. A. Murphy and Joseph A. Burgess, eds., *Justification by Faith: Lutheran and Catholics in Dialogue VII*, (Minneapolis: Augsburg Publishing House, 1985), 23. Hereafter cited as Anderson, *Justification.*

76 Bainton, *Here I Stand*, p. 65.

But, while he was teaching in Wittenburg University, Luther had a new understanding of justification from reading Paul's Epistle to the Romans and studying Augustine's writing. Luther realized that the righteousness of God is the righteousness which is given to us so that we may meet the requirement for justification. Righteousness is God's gift rather than a righteousness which belongs to God. It depends more on the reckoning of God than on the essence itself. God pronounces the sinner righteous, not on the basis of the sinner's work but through the righteousness of Christ which is imputed to the sinner. God sees the sinner as one with Christ, forgiving and considering the sinners to be righteous for Christ's sake. [77] This changed the whole complexion of "the judge":

> Where, then, is the judge, sitting upon the rainbow to condemn sinners? He is still the judge. He must judge, as truth judges error and light darkness; but in judging he suffers with those whom he must condemn and feels himself with them subject to condemnation.[78]

Luther now saw that it was God who met the precondition, graciously giving sinners what they require if they are to be justified. Human receives justifications only through faith, that is, by believing and trusting in Jesus Christ. Faith is the work and gift of God given to human in justification. This faith unites the believer to Christ and brings him/her closer to God personally.[79]

Luther's conviction that faith alone justifies without works was in severe disagreement to the Roman Catholic Church practice of indulgences. Rejecting the idea that human acts, such as the purchase of indulgences, could become the agent of attaining salvation, Luther argues that believing and trusting in the saving acts of Jesus Christ alone was the necessary and sufficient condition of salvation. The Roman Catholic countered Luther's view in the Council of Trent where "justification" was interpreted to mean both the beginning of the Christian life and its continuation and growth, and alleged that

77 Bainton, *Here I Stand*, p. 65; McGrath, *Christian Theology*, p. 373.

78 Bainton, *Here I Stand*, p. 62.

79 McGrath, *Christian Theology*, pp. 373-4; Paul Althaus, *The Theology of Martin Luther* (Philadelphia: Fortress Press, 1981), pp. 230-231.

Luther was suggesting that simply trusting in God was the basis of the entire Christian life, thereby criticizing Luther's justifying faith.[80]

However, Luther does not reject the necessity of good works in justification. While he maintains that faith alone justifies without works, this faith is evident in good works. He often uses the biblical image of the good tree to illustrate his point.

> We confess that good works must follow faith, yes, not only must, but follow voluntarily, just as a good tree not only must produce good fruits, but does so freely (Matt. 7:18).
>
> But good works come from a person who has already been justified beforehand by faith, just as good fruits come from a tree which is already good beforehand by nature.[81]
>
> Works only reveals faith…they show that we have been justified, just as his fruits show that a man (sic) is a Christian and believes in Christ, since he does not have a feigned faith and life before men (sic). For the work indicates whether I have faith. I conclude, therefore, that he is righteous, when I see that he does good works.[82]

To sum up, Luther holds that "justification by faith" never negates good works while good works alone can never merit justification. Being the consequence of faith, good works testify true faith and believers are thus encouraged to do good works because where there are no works, there is no faith as "true faith is not idle."[83]

4.5.2. Calvin's understanding of "justification by faith", "deeds" and "rewards": Regarding "justification by faith" Calvin followed Luther to a large extend. Calvin states:

---

80 McGrath, *Christian Theology*, p. 379.

81 Martin Luther, "Thesis Concerning Faith and Law," trans. and ed. by Lewis W. Spitz, in *Luther's Works,* Vol. 34, (Philadelphia: Muhlenberg Press, 1960), p. 111. Hereafter cited as *Luther's Works*, 34.

82 Martin Luther, "The Disputation Concerning Justification," in *Luther's Works,* 34, p. 161.

83 Luther, "The Disputation Concerning Justification," in *Luther's Works,* 34, p. 183.

> [J]ustified by faith is he (sic) who, excluded from the righteousness of works, grasps righteousness of Christ through faith, and clothed in it, appears in God's sight not as a sinner but as a righteous man (sic).[84]

Calvin's understanding of "justification by faith alone" therefore molded his concept of "judgment" and "rewards" and he stressed emphatically that "under God's judgment we must not put any trust in works, or glory in any esteem of them."[85] In rejecting rewards as the merits of works, he reflects Augustine's assertion, "When God, crowning our merits, crowns nothing else but His own gifts to us."[86] Commenting on Augustine, he states:

> How often does this thought recur in Augustine: "God does not crown our merits but his own gifts"; "we call 'rewards' not what are due our merits, but what are rendered for graces already bestowed"![87]

While Calvin clearly rejects rewards as solely the merits of works but an expression of God's grace, his position was quite similar with Luther who never regards "justification by faith" as negating good works. Calvin states:

> [The knowledge of Christ] is a doctrine...of life...[I]t must enter our heart and pass into our daily living, and so transform us into itself that it may not be unfruitful for us.[88]

> [W]hen we rule out reliance upon works...we do not forbid him from undergirding and strengthening this faith by signs of the divine benevolence toward him...[M]uch more is this true of the grace of good works, which shows that the Spirit of adoption has been given to us.[89]

---

84 Calvin, *Institutes,* pp. 726-7.

85 Calvin, *Institutes* III.14.18, p. 785.

86 "Letter of Augustine to Sixtus (194, 5, 19), " in *The Faith of the Early Fathers, Volume Three,* selected and translated by William A. Jurgens, (Bangalore: TPI, 1984), p. 11.

87 Calvin, *Institutes* II.5.2, p. 318; see also *Institutes* III.18.5, pp. 825-7.

88 Calvin, *Institutes* III.6.4, p. 688.

89 Calvin, *Institutes* III.14.18, p. 785.

Hence, after stressing "works" as the consequence and not the cause of justification, and rewards as "received" because of God's grace and not to be "claimed", he encouraged believers to do good works as God promises to recompense them.

> [Reward] is a compensation for their miseries, tribulations, slanders, etc....[It] is promised for good works to relieve the weakness of our flesh by some comfort but not to puff up our hearts with vainglory.[90]

> [T]hose good works which [God] has bestowed upon us the Lord calls "ours," and testifies they not only are acceptable to him but also will have their reward. It is our duty in return to be aroused by so great a promise, to take courage not to weary in well-doing...and to receive God's great kindness with true gratefulness.[91]

> But how shall we transmit them (i.e., store their treasures in heaven)? Surely, by providing for the needs of the poor; whatever is paid out to them, the Lord reckons as given to himself....For what is devoted to our brothers out of the duty of love is deposited in the Lord's hand. He, as he is a faithful custodian, will one day repay it with plentiful interest.[92]

While maintaining the "eschatological" significance of good works, Calvin also holds that God's promise was not only confined to the Last Day. Even before believers were bestowed this reward in the last judgment, the souls of the believers – which does not perish or sleep in death - enjoyed "provisional blessedness"[93] upon death:

> [T]he souls of the pious, having ended the toil of their warfare, enter into blessed rest, where in glad expectation they await the enjoyment of promised glory, and so all things are held in suspense until Christ the Redeemer appear. The lot of the

90 Calvin, *Institutes* III.18.4, p. 825.

91 Calvin, *Institutes* III.15.3, p. 790.

92 Calvin, *Institutes* III.18.6, p. 827.

93 Heinrich Quistorp, *Calvin's Doctrine of the Last Things*, (London: Lutterworth Press, 1955), p. 81.

> reprobate is...to be held in chains until they are dragged to the punishment appointed for them.[94]

So, in this state of "provisional blessedness", the souls of the believers await the glorious fulfillment of God's promise. For Calvin, the "final coming of Christ"[95] to resurrect the dead will be followed by the final judgment when the believers will enjoy the promise of God in its fullness. This "final coming of Christ" was the object of the believers' blessed hope which must sustain the believers until its completion.

We can conclude this section by asserting that the grace of God is paramount in Calvin's thought. So, in clasping them under the theme, "The way we receive grace" in his *Institutes*, Calvin relates justification of the believers with the second coming of Christ, the resurrection of the dead and final judgment: being an extension and hopeful culmination of the benefits of believers that fall under the scheme of grace, it is an eschatological event. Calvin's "eschatological-orientedness" can be represented by what he called a "double grace": instead of a Judge in heaven we have a gracious God because we are reconciled to God through Christ's blamelessness, and we are empowered to cultivate blamelessness and purity of life as we are sanctified by Christ's spirit.[96]

---

94 Calvin, *Institutes* III.25.6, p. 998.

95 We must note that Calvin makes a remarkable distinction between the Last Day, which signifies the "final coming of Christ" and the "last days", which refers to all time between Christ's earthly ministry and the last judgment. He writes:

> [T]he whole New Testament time, from the point that Christ appeared to us with the preaching of his Gospel even to the Day of Judgment, is designated by..."the last times", "the last days."
>
> [T]his age of ours is designated in the Scripture by...the "last days", the "last times," that no one should delude himself with a vain expectation of some new doctrine or revelation.

Calvin, *Institutes* IV.8.7, p. 1155; IV.18.20, p. 1447. In the second instance, Calvin's main argument concerns the finality of Christ as a means of grace for the believers.

96 Calvin, *Institutes* III.11.1, p. 725. Quistorp argue that Calvin's "whole theology is eschatologically oriented [which is evident] from the conscious coordination

Conclusion

In this chapter, we highlight various factors that influenced the formulation of the PCI Confession of Faith. We have asserted that the Westminster Confession of Faith and other derivative doctrinal statements were ultimately drawn from Calvin's *Institutes of the Christian Religion* which makes Calvin's *Institutes* indispensable to the PCI Confession of Faith and so, must be seen in the light of it. Stating that the concept of "judgment according to one's deeds" was the main theme of Article X, we maintain that it is not antithetical to the Reformation's watchword: justification by faith.

We particularly look at how Calvin integrates "faith" and "work" under the grand scheme of the grace of God so that "justification by faith" finds expression and fruition in good works. Believer's good works were accepted by God so that they will be recompensed in the final judgment. And the grace of God is an assurance that "those who slept in the Lord" (I Thess 4:13) were justified, and were thereby in a state of provisional blessedness, awaiting the fulfillment of God's glorious promise which will be revealed in the second coming of Christ. Therefore, the second coming of Christ, the resurrection of the dead and the final judgment will be the ultimate expression of the grace of God upon the believers.

In the next chapter, we shall give a general appraisal of Article X. Looking at the popular rendering of "judgment" that caused anxiety and division among the Mizo Christians, we shall expound the concept of "judgment" in the light of "hope in Christ." Enquiring how various eschatological themes should be held in complement with soteriology, we shall integrate our observations to draw its significance for contemporary Mizo Christian spirituality.

---

of faith and hope which it discloses." Heinrich Quistorp, *Calvin's Doctrine of the Last Things*, p. 11.

Chapter 5

General Appraisal of Article X of the Presbyterian Church of India's Confession of Faith

If for this life only we have hoped in Christ,
we are of all people most to be pitied.
1 Corinthians 15:19
So let us not grow weary in doing what is right,
for we will reap at harvest time, if we do not give up.
Ephesians 6:9

In chapter 2, we have explored the biblical concept of "judgment according to the deeds" and mentioned that its rootedness in the justice of God inspired faith that looks beyond this world and this life, giving rise to Christian eschatology. In chapter 3, we asserted that Mizo Christian spirituality was permeated by eschatological worldview where the concept of "judgment according to the deeds" was central. In chapter 4, we mentioned that the concept of "judgment according to the deeds" in the Last Day, which was the main theme of Article X of the PCI Confession of Faith, was not antithetical to the Reformation watchword: justification by faith.

This chapter will explore the significance of the PCI Confession of Faith Article X for contemporary Mizo Christian eschatological imagination. Looking at the popular depiction of "judgment" that caused anxiety and confusion among the Mizo Christians, we will expound the concept of "judgment" in the light of "hope in Christ" and see the implications and challenges that Article X poses for the Mizo Christians.

5.1 Apocalyptic Millennialist's Concept of "Judgment" in Mizoram

Although Christian fundamentalism, with its millennial obsession, was often associated with American Christians,[1] a vivid portrayal of the last judgment often resembling fundamentalism has always captured the eschatological imagination of Mizo Christians. Since the revival movements aroused a sense of the imminent return of Jesus Christ, expectation of millennial reign was popularized by evangelists and preachers in Mizoram for a long time. Reflecting upon the prevalence of millennialism, Chuauthuama even remarked that millennial reign of Christ should be called "popular eschatology" as it was not an official eschatology of the church but was still a popular view.[2] Millennialism literally refers to the view, basing on the Book of Revelation, that Christ will inaugurate a one-thousand year reign of the saints on earth before the last judgment. Premillennialists expected that the second coming of Jesus Christ will take place before, and thus initiate, a thousand-year Kingdom of God on earth while postmillennialists believed that Christ's second coming would take place after earth's millennial age.[3]

---

1 It was remarked that millennial speculations have become "America's favourite pastime." Wilkinson, *Christian Eschatology,* p. 4.

2 Chuauthuama, "Hun Hnuhnung Thlir Dan," pp. 63-4.

3 Richard A. Landes, "Millennialism in the Western World," and Robert K. Whalen, "Postmillennialism," "Premillennialism," in *The Encyclopedia of Millennialism and Millennial Movements*, ed. by Richard A. Landes, (New York: Routledge, 2000), pp. 453, 578, 584.

As millennial expectation gripped many Mizo Christians, apocalyptic sectarian groups[4] who may be described as "Christian fundamentalists" started taking root in many parts of Mizoram. According to A. J. Frykholm, Christian fundamentalists "found themselves a part of the cosmic story of rapture and tribulation that helped them interpret their place and activity in the world. They discovered their roles through the interpretation of this apocalyptic narrative."[5] In Mizoram, some common themes or "apocalyptic narrative" such sectarian groups usually shared in their teaching were the redemption of the body and of being "chosen" - to enjoy Christ's millennial reign on earth or to avoid an impending doom and judgment of God, or to escape the tyranny of "the beast" or the Antichrist. This conviction usually compelled them to leave their homes and kindred to settle somewhere as a community or at least, to leave the "visible" church which usually connotes the Presbyterian Church.

Accordingly, Khuangtuahthanga and his brother Challianchana formed an eschatological community called *Lalpa Kohhran Thar* or "The New Church of the Lord", and regarded themselves as the first fruits of Christ's millennial reign. They believed that God had chosen them in place of the now forsaken Israel of the Bible and regarded their leaders as "the new Moses." Under the leadership of Chana, who had 7 wives and 38 children, the community settled at Baktawng near Aizawl. Chana's son Zionnghaka has around 39 wives and 94 children, and this community is the most vibrant of the apocalyptic

---

4 In chapter three, we have mentioned that the central message of Khawliantlira, who formed the first sectarian group in Mizoram, was the millennial reign of Christ. Vanlalchhuanga believed that all the subsequent sectarian groups also take over this theme. Vanlalchhuanga, *An Zirtirnate leh an Chanchin*, Revised and Enlarged (Venghnuai: Gosen Home, 2010), p.v. Hereafter cited as Chhuanga, *An Zirtirnate.* Lalsawma mentioned ten major apocalyptic sects in Mizoram and the period they started to get active: Khawliantlira – 1913; Lalnghenga – 1937; Khuangtuahthanga – 1942; Challianchana – 1969; Chala and Darnghaka – 1955; Zathangvunga – 1965; Thanchhuma – 1966; Vanawia – 1977; Lalzawna – 1986; Rorelliana – 1990. Lalsawma, *Kristian Thurin Zirna*, p. 313.

5 Amy Johnson Frykholm, *Rapture Culture: Left Behind in Evangelical America*, (Oxford: Oxford University Press, Inc., 2004), p. 16.

sects in Mizoram till today. Another sect headed by Vanawia settled at Sangau, a remote place in southern Mizoram with the belief that they were the chosen few who will usher in Christ's millennial reign on earth, just as Jesus chose only twelve disciples in his ministry. Another sectarian leader, Vanlalzawna taught that a huge rock will roll down from the East that will wreak havoc in its path and urged his followers to sell their houses and lands in different towns and sub-towns of Mizoram and migrate to smaller villages where the impact will be less severe. Perceiving institutionalized state or government as agent of "the beast", adherents severed their ties by giving up their government jobs and by refraining from sending their children to school.[6] Even today, major events and political developments almost always motivate some sections of Mizo Christians to suspect a "conspiracy" regarding the appearance of the Antichrist before Christ's millennial reign and this also directly or indirectly influences members of the Mizoram Presbyterian Church.

The most recent occurrence was during the last national census in 2011. Information for National Population Register was gathered, which was to be used to issue a 12-digit Unique Identification (UID) number to all registered Indians by Unique Identification Authority of India. Some "apocalyptic-minded" Mizo Christians, basing their reading on Rev 13:16-17, regarded this "Unique Identification" as the sign of the Antichrist that the book of Revelation described. Around 1355 families refused to be included in the census. Mizoram Presbyterian Church even issued a statement regarding the true nature of the census, explaining the idea behind the introduction of UID and its lack of threat for true believers.[7] Afterward the Church released a booklet titled *I am not afraid of the beast* in 2012 and 2013, followed by another statement in 2014 as many were still "afraid" of having the UID.[8]

---

6 See Lalbiaktluanga, "Mizorama Zirtirna Hrang Hrang Thlirna," in *Mizo Miziaa Pathian Thu*, (Aizawl: Synod Publication Board, 1998), pp. 72-3. Hereafter cited as Biaktluanga, "Mizorama Zirtirna"; Lalsawma, *Revivals – The Mizo Way*, pp. 187-190. Chhuanga, *An Zirtirnate,* pp. 39-41, 80-2.

7 "Chhiarpui leh Sakawlh," *Synod Newsletter,* 28/ 320, (June, 2010), p. 1.

8 "Tunlaia Sakawlh Hlaute Thil Hlauh Hi," *Synod Newsletter,* 28/ 365, (February, 2014), p. 1.

Although the allegation of UID as a mark of allegiance to "the beast" may seem far-fetched, the pervasiveness of this "apocalyptic world view" is best highlighted by the resolution of the Synod Meeting of Mizoram Presbyterian Church during the same period. In 2010, the General Assembly of the Presbyterian Church of India wanted a consensus on whether to become a full member of the World Council of Churches (WCC) - long considered the Antichrist or "the beast" by various sectarian groups and denominational churches,[9] and asked the opinion of the eight units of the PCI including Mizoram Synod. The matter was discussed by the Mizoram Synod Meeting in December 2010. As opinion differed, the Synod Meeting sought the opinion of the different Presbyteries.[10] In the Presbytery Meetings, the matter was further discussed and 14 Presbyteries wanted to join the WCC while 29 Presbyteries decided against joining the WCC,

---

9 According to Vanlalzawna, the WCC will give a secret identity to all its members which is the mark of allegiance to "the beast." Lalbiakmawia, the leader of "The Holy Church", teaches that WCC was the harlot that was described in Rev.17:1. Chhuanga, *An Zirtirnate,* pp. 58, 109-13.

When the PCI considered joining the WCC as a full members, Lungmuana wrote an article highlighting the true nature of the WCC and attempted to dispel five main allegations which usually alarmed and cause panic among many church members:

a. that the Roman Catholic Church is a member of the WCC; b. that the WCC is the beast [basing on Daniel 7:3 and 17:1]; c. that World Religions Congress is a member of the WCC; d. that the WCC and European Common Market (ECM) have joined hands. The things produced by ECM can only be bought by those people who bear the number 666; e. that the WCC is [interpreted as] a person of Lawlessness (II Thess. 2:4), the Awful Horror (Matt. 24:15) and the Harlot (Rev. 12:1).

K. Lungmuana, "Merits and Demerits of Being a member of the WCC," *Presbyterian Review*, 16/52, (Oct-Dec., 2008), p. 45. In Mizoram, the Seventh Day Adventist considered the Pope as "the beast" for making the church to observe Sunday instead of the Sabbath and the allegation that the Roman Catholic Church is a member of the WCC amounted to saying that the WCC is "the beast." Chhuanga, *An Zirtirnate,* pp. 4-5, 183; see also P. C.Biaksiama, *666: Sakawlh leh a Chhinchhiahna*, (Aizawl: Christian Research Centre, 2010), pp. 9,16, 83-94. Hereafter cited as Biaksiama, *666;* cf. Chuauthuama, "Hun Hnuhnung Thlir Dan," p. 54; Vanlalauva, *Hun Hnuhnung Thu*, p. 284.

10 *Minutes of the 2010 Synod Meeting, Gen. 77*, (Aizawl: Synod Press, 2010), p. 64.

fearing that church members were not convinced of the "true" nature of the WCC. On that basis, Mizoram Synod Meeting held in 2011 decided against joining the WCC as full member, which further prevents the Presbyterian Church of India from joining the WCC as of now.[11]

This clearly shows that fundamentalist ideology is strong among the Mizo and that many take the Bible literally to match current events with biblical prophecy and predict the near future, particularly regarding the approaching "tribulation" (Mark 13:19, 24).[12] Most importantly, we can see the teachings of past apocalyptic sectarian groups in Mizoram being reinterpreted and fused with Western fundamentalism whose "apocalyptic mindset" is promoted through books,[13] newsletters and magazines, the internet and television channels like Miracle Net, the God channel and the local Mizo channels.

In this apocalyptic mindset, an important tenet for vindication in the final judgment consists of being conscious about the Antichrist so that true believers can "resist the forces of evil" and "suffer in God's name." Even this awareness and alertness itself became judgmental as it demands response. The fear of negligence and ignorance that this expectation invokes, to some extent, became a "control mechanism". Many Christians believe that the reign of the coming Antichrist will be marked by a time of earthly travail which will be escaped by the "Elect" through the Rapture. This belief in the Rapture largely eclipses hope in resurrection of the dead as the Rapture is mostly concerned with those who are still alive.[14]

---

11 *Minutes of the 2011 Synod Meeting, Gen. 44*, (Aizawl: Synod Press, 2011), p. 51.

12 Biaksiama, *666*, p. 106.

13 Chuauthuama, "Hun Hnuhnung Thlir Dan," pp. 46-7, 54.

14 One popular song among the Presbyterian Youth Fellowship (KTP) in Mizoram, compiled by a Seventh Day Adventist pastor, solely focus on the Rapture, not on the resurrection, and end with this rapturous lines: "When the saved are 'being caught up,' You do take me along too." This does not mean that the youth members considered the Rapture as viable way of imagining eschatology or that they had an apocalyptic mindset. But it clearly shows the problem we identified in chapter three that due to a lack of the concept of "resurrection of the dead" in the traditional Mizo "eschatology", vindication

At the same time, bold predictions and vivid descriptions about the approaching "judgment" also left a large number of the Mizo Christians perplexed and anxious. And for some, it makes all "the doctrines" of the last things ambiguous and some even find the whole eschatological concept a futile speculation and very unconvincing.

5.2 Doctrinal Affirmation in the Midst of Ambiguity: An Urgent Theological Task

Despite the growing skepticism and ambiguity, apocalyptic preoccupation is still vibrant in the Mizo Christian imagination. Therefore, the question as to what kind of theology or faith affirmation the Mizo Christians need to meet their deep eschatological concern becomes crucial. Another important question is, "Why does the notion of millennialism continue to be vibrant?" According to Lalbiaktluanga, the close affinity between the Mizo concept of *Pialral* and the interpretation of the millennial reign may be an important factor behind the popularity of millennialism.[15] If so, does this connote a friction between Mizo culture and the official "eschatology" that the church received through her doctrinal affirmation? This is an important question when we consider the difference of opinion regarding millennialism with the Mizoram Presbyterian Church.

In 1992, Synod Publication Board (SPB)[16] decided to bring out a book on eschatology to clarify the Church's position.[17] After a year, SPB decided to organize a seminar on the subject which will be compiled as a book.[18] Later, four Presbyterian ministers were assigned to write a paper on four topics for the seminar.[19] After one year, the

---

before the resurrection - either immediately after death or through some kind of Rapture, always lingers in Mizo eschatological imagination.

15 Biaktluanga, "Mizorama Zirtirna," p. 80. We must note that among the Mizo there is a close connection between the concept of reigning, ruling and judging. Rulers and judges were usually one and the same and millennial reign largely presuppose ruling and therefore judging.

16 Synod Publication Board is the publishing unit of the Mizoram Presbyterian Church.

17 *Minutes of the SPB Meeting on 22nd Jan. 1992.* (Cyclostyled).

18 *Minutes of the SPB Meeting on 17th Nov. 1993.* (Cyclostyled).

19 *Minutes of the SPB Meeting on 18th Jan. 1994.* (Cyclostyled).

SPB, which now became Synod Literature and Publication Board (SL&PB) fixed the date of the seminar to be 29th September, 1995.[20] Subsequently, SL&PB reviewed the seminar and decided that some papers need to be reworked and another seminar may be held, if needed, before they were published as a book.[21] After one year, it was decided that the resource persons and the editor of the SL&PB should consult each other to finish the book.[22] But the book was never published.

Chuauthuama, one of the resource persons in the seminar, opines that it was to the best of interests that the book never came out because Pastors and Church Elders who attended the seminar have different convictions regarding millennialism and debated passionately. Trying to bring out a book on the subject can be highly divisive, especially if it was to be taken as the Church's official position.[23] R. Lalthanmawia, another resource person, states that some Presbyterian Ministers were stern advocates in the seminar though millennialism was never the official position of the Reformed Church.[24]

In the light of this as well as our previous observations, we can say that there is a need to have an eschatological affirmation that is not only rooted in the Bible and the church's traditions and confessional statements but one which takes the past culture of the Mizo seriously while truly addressing the contemporary context of Mizo Christianity. Particularly, there is a need to have an eschatological affirmation that is consistent with soteriology, where the balance between faith and hope, justification and judgment, grace and merits, this world and the next can be maintained.

5.2.1. A brief consideration of Article X in the context of Mizo Christianity: Considering these "needs", can Article X be reckoned as a proper affirmation of faith when it comes to meeting the eschatological yearning of the Mizo Christians, given that almost

20 *Minutes of the SL&PB Meeting on 2nd August 1995.* (Cyclostyled).

21 *Minutes of the SL&PB Meeting on 23rd Oct. 1995.* (Cyclostyled).

22 *Minutes of the SL&PB Meeting on 25th July 1996.* (Cyclostyled).

23 Interview with Chuauthuama, 2nd Sept. 2013.

24 Interview with R. Lalthanmawia, 14th Sept. 2013.

all sectarian groups in Mizoram seceded from the Presbyterian Church?[25]

We can make the following observations as we analyze this Article:

i. As seen earlier, Article X was not a contextual formulation but an adaptation of Western eschatology in the spirit of the Westminster Confession of Faith. This Confession and its derivative doctrinal statements were ultimately derived from Calvin's *Institutes of the Christian Religion* and represented Calvin's theology as well as Reformed Christianity. This means that Calvin's *Institutes* was also foundational to Article X and must be seen in the light of it.

But, Article X lost much of its "original" meaning when it was abridged for the "young" Indian Churches. As Calvin's systematic and thorough treatment of Christian "truth" was condensed and broken down into a self-contained unit or separate Articles, Calvin's concept of "double grace" was split up and compartmentalized in the Ten Articles of Faith of the PCI. However, as Schwobel rightly says, "there are considerable risks…in isolating [eschatology] from its connection with other articles of Christian faith….[and] the doctrinal scheme of Christianity."[26] And justification "now" somewhat became antithetical with resurrection and judgment "later" in Mizo Christian concept, while Calvin holds them together under the grand scheme of God's grace for the believers.

ii. As the brief PCI Confession of Faith fails to bring out the original intention, the concept of "Last Day" in Article X is particularly ambiguous. This word can suggest a day of resurrection, of judgment, of acquittal for the believers and of condemnation and punishment for sinners. In popular understanding, it denotes "the end of the world" which corresponded to the original Mizo rendering *nikin ni* [27] that stressed the consummation or the end of days.

25 Chhuanga, *An Zirtirnate,* pp. 34,37, 46-7, 63, 72,96; cf. Vanlalauva, *Hun Hnuhnung Thu*, pp. 325-6.

26 Christoph Schwobel, "Last things first?" in *The Future as God's Gift: Exploration in Christian Theology*, ed. by David Fergusson and Marvel Sarot, (Edinburgh: T&T Clark, 2000) pp. 237-8. Hereafter cited as Schwobel, "Last things".

27 This translation in 1925 was incidentally preceded by a revival where the theme of the second coming and the end of the world was prevalent. Though

Moreover, Article X can be more Christocentric, and have continuity and consistency with soteriology, if the "Last Day" was qualified with the second coming of Jesus Christ as was suggested by the Nicene Creed and Article V of the PCI Confession of Faith.[28] This can portray the second coming of Christ to judge "the quick and the death" as the culmination of a soterio-eschatological event which begins with the life, death and resurrection of Jesus, and ends with the final vindication of believers. This will also stress the "once and for all"-ness of the Christ event where the forces of evil and death were defeated definitely, thereby negating the concept of "final struggles still to come and still undecided"[29] that lingers in the imagination of Mizo apocalyptic sects. Above all, this will put Article X within a proper framework because "the pattern of Christian hope will always be a pattern based on the matrix of the Christ event."[30]

iii. Similarly, a more definite word than simply "the Last Day" can show that Article X refutes such particular stance like apocalyptic millennialism[31] which Calvin never endorsed but that caught the imagination of the Mizo Christians and caused division among

---

it was changed into *ni hnuhnungah* in subsequent translations which connote a final stage more than the end, the original translation seems to stick on in the common understanding.

28 The Nicene Creed states, "He shall come again with glory to judge the quick and the dead". And Article V of the PCI Confession affirmed that "he shall come again to raise the dead and to judge the world". According to Lalthanmawia, Article X does not contain other eschatological issues such as second coming of Jesus, end of the world, the millennium reign of Christ and heaven and hell. While the second coming of Christ is affirmed in the Article V in the section concerning Jesus Christ, the other eschatological topics may be overlook as secondary importance for new believers. Lalthanmawia, *Reinterpretation of Calvin.*

29 Moltmann, *Coming of God*, p. 233.

30 Schwobel, "Last things," p. 237.

31 According to Venema, acknowledging that the final judgment will occur soon after the resurrection implies that this judgment will be a single event, which will negate the dispensational millennialist position for whom two or more distinct judgments are necessary. Cornelis P. Venema, *The Promise of the Future*, (Edinburgh: The Banner of Truth Trust, 2000), pp. 393-4. Hereafter cited as Venema, *Promise of the Future.*

them.[32] This notion may be incited by the word "shall be judged" in Article X which slightly differs with the SIUC *Confession* which has "shall receive". The *Shorter Catechism* and the *Summary of Faith* do not mention judging or receiving and asserted that believers shall be openly acknowledged and acquitted in the Day of Judgment. The word "shall be judged" can suggest an ongoing trial though appearance before judgment seat presupposes some kind of verdict. Though we do not know why "judged" was preferred, the word "receive" may be more definite and in line with Reformed traditions which suggest an execution of judgment for the believers basing on God's grace, which is an open acquittal. It may also bring more clarity regarding the Church's stance towards various concepts of millennialism.

iv. Regarding the affirmation that sinners shall suffer the punishment due to their sins and that believers shall be received into glory, questions can be raised about the period between death and the last judgment, on which the Article is silent. As the "Last Day" seems to imply the future, probably a distant one, believers tend to be more concerned with the immediate condition of those who are dead. Similarly, unlike the Westminster Confession, Article X does not include the theological validation, i.e., the necessity of a day of judgment, which tends to serve as an encouragement for believers as well as a caution against sinning. Therefore, it fails to bridge the gap between the present deeds and its future implication as forcefully as the Westminster Confession does.

To sum up, we can say that Article X is not adequate or definite in itself to address the eschatological concern of Mizo Christians. And given the diverse themes and understanding of eschatology today, it will be difficult to have a concise and definite formulation which can attend to all the issues and concerns that eschatology

---

32 Largely popularized by the workers of North-East India General (NEIG) Mission after 1919, "millennial reign" caught the fancy of Mizo Christians so much that most sectarian groups who left the Presbyterian Church of Mizoram were inclined toward this teaching. Vanlalauva, *Hun Hnuhnung Thu,* p. 325. Thanmawia states that the millennium reign of Christ is the neglected part of eschatology in the Reformed theology and that Calvin's successors never expect the millennium reign of Christ to be literally established on earth and hence, majority of the Reformed theologians are branded as 'a-millenarians'. Lalthanmawia, *Reinterpretation of Calvin.*

generates. For instance, a relevant eschatological affirmation cannot reject millennialism because it is so pervasive in Mizo Christian eschatological imagination. Although millennialism was not officially endorsed in the tradition of the Reformed churches, it was maintained that holding this view personally was not prohibited as long it was beneficial for the believer's spiritual life.[33] We shall see more of this in the next section.

But, while acknowledging the inadequacy of Article X as well as the need for openness, some of these issues like the immediate state of the soul after death can be addressed by expanding it in line with the *Shorter Catechism* or the *Summary of Faith*. And Article X must be expounded in the light of Calvin's *Institutes* so that the concept of judgment must be consistent with the doctrine of justification by faith. Its implication will be that "eschatology" in Article X would not be confined to the "Last Day" of the future general eschatology. Eschatology can embrace the present as the "last days", thereby taking individual event into account. Thus, the last judgment will be the consummation of the process of justification.

5.2.2. Towards a meaningful convergence of worldviews - the challenges:

i. The challenge of cultural tradition: Although the pre-Christian Mizo concept of life after death was accommodative to the Western Christian eschatological concept, there is a vibrant interpretation of eschatology which does not conform to the Church doctrine right from the time of the early Mizo Christians. This was identified as apocalyptic millennialism in the previous section, a specific form of millenarianism. In recent times, social scientists have attempted to understand millenarianism outside of its original religious foundations. According to James Rinehart, incidences of millenarian anticipation

> are not exclusively dependent upon Jewish or Christian traditions of religious prophecy or…traditional worldview….

---

33 See Vanlalauva, *Hun Hnuhnung Thu*, p. 277; *Kristian Tlangau Centenary Project: Kum 1911-2011 chhung atanga Editorial leh Zawhna leh Chhanna Lawrkhawm*, (Aizawl: SL&PB, 2011), pp. 370, 389.

> Despite their diverse cultural sources, the conditions present at the time of their eruption are notably alike. Society is undergoing rapid change. In addition, long-standing cultural traditions are systematically invalidated by seemingly more powerful forces generally delivered by the invasion of Western culture into the region. As a result, the peoples of these communities are experiencing mass alienation and insecurity. Under such disruptive circumstances, powerful modern messiahs have emerged around the world.[34]

If seen from this perspective, the apocalyptic millennialism of Tlira and subsequent sectarian groups can denote, to a certain extent, the inherent friction between Mizo culture and the Western mindset which Christianity promotes. It also portrays the tension between traditional Mizo concept of *pialral*[35] and Christian soteriology. Hence, instead of "invoking" and "imposing" doctrinal "correctness" on eschatological imagination basing on Church doctrinal exposition, cultural and traditional background influence must be taken into consideration. And for this, the culturally-rooted eschatology that finds expression in the indigenous Mizo hymns need to be valued as an indispensable tool for a relevant Mizo Christian eschatology. As Lalsawma rightly says, "Christian singing was a new and exciting form of adventure into the unknown and the unseen world."[36]

ii. The philosophical and scientific challenges: Assuming Calvin's *Institutes* and the Mizo cultural background as significant for a relevant Mizo eschatological imagination poses another question. Why do we need to embrace an eschatological doctrine that was largely determined by the worldview of the past today? If

34 James F. Rinehart, *Apocalyptic Faith and Political Violence: Prophets of Terror*, (New York: Palgrave Macmillan, 2006), pp. 3-4; see chap. 3, footnote 99 where we noted the Mizo revivalists' longing for "new land."

35 See chapter 3, 3. Christian soteriology particularly negates the stipulation for entitlement to *pialral*.

36 Lalsawma, *Revivals – The Mizo Way*, p. 127. He states that translated hymns in Western tunes were mostly sung by early Mizo Christians to maintain their new identity before indigenous tunes and hymns became popular as a result of the third revival. Interview with Lalsawma, 10th Sept. 2013. Cf. chapter 3.3.4.

this question is approached from "philosophical naturalism"[37] or a "scientific worldview" which "secular" education promotes among the Mizo, problems and challenges abound. The problems and the challenges they pose to eschatology may be fairly summarized by Polkinghorne who states that science

> presents us with the picture of a universe that, despite its present fruitfulness, will eventually end in the futility of cosmic collapse or decay. This reliable prediction poses a sharp question to theology concerning how the latter conceives of the ultimate fulfilment of God's creation.[38]

And in the attempt to negotiate scientific and philosophical worldview with eschatology, the answers can differ. Polkinghorne insists that a convincing Christian eschatology "will have to include elements of both continuity and discontinuity in the linkages that it makes between the present universe and its destiny beyond its death."[39] Webster asserts that eschatological belief "takes the form of confidence in the promises of God, a confidence whose certainty cannot be replaced by an act of intellectual or spiritual or political possession of the object of hope."[40] For Ted Peters, the transformation of the natural world "will have to come courtesy of a creative act of God. No one can predict a creative act of God; hence it will remain invisible to present scientific eyes."[41] For Tyron Inbody, what and why Christian believes in "individual survival is not dependent on philosophical arguments. Belief is rooted in Christology. On the basis

37 Nichols, *Death and Afterlife*, pp. 11-3.

38 John Polkinghorne, *The God of Hope and the End of the World*, (New Haven: Yale University Press, 2002), p.xviii. Hereafter cited as Polkinghorne, *The God of Hope.*

39 Polkinghorne, *The God of Hope,* p. xviii.

40 Webster, *Word and Church*, p. 275.

41 Ted Peters, "What is to come," in *Resurrection: Theological and Scientific Assessment,* ed. by Ted Peters, Robert John Russell and Michael Welker, (Michigan: William B. Eerdmans Publishing Co., 2002), p.xi. Hereafter cited as Peters, "What is to come".

of the resurrection of Jesus, the church affirms individual survival as one part of our hope."[42]

Despite the different approaches to the question regarding the convergence of traditional Christian eschatology with scientific and philosophical worldview, all these answers affirmed this assertion: it is because Christians hope in the promise of God. And this hope makes sense for Christians. Paul said, "For in hope we were saved. Now hope that is seen is not hope. For who hope for what is seen? But if we hope for what we do not see, we wait for it with patience" (Rom. 8.24-5). Therefore, as Christians hope in the promise of God in the past, Christians still, and will continue hoping until the fulfillment of this promise. In the next section, we shall examine the concept of "judgment according to the deeds" from the perspective of Christian hope to see its relevance for the Mizo Christian context today.

5.3 Interpreting and Reaffirming the Concept of "Judgment According to the Deeds"

Despite the apparent inadequacy of Article X, the notion of "judgment according to the deeds" which was its main theme can still be reckoned as an indispensable aspect in Mizo Christian eschatological affirmation. This concept is a key element as it was biblically attested and affirmed in the traditional creeds and confessions of the church. As seen, the concept of judgment was also present in the pre-Christian Mizo eschatology and continues to be a dominant theme in Mizo Christian eschatological imagination. In fact, almost all the sectarian groups have been preoccupied with the concept of millennial reign and judgment in one way or the other.[43] But given the problems mentioned in previous chapters regarding grace and merit, faith and work, how can Mizo Christians hold the concept of "judgment" together with the doctrine of "justification by faith"?

5.3.1. Interpreting "judgment" in the light of "hope in Christ": We have asserted that the biblical concept of judgment is rooted in the

42 Inbody, *The Faith Of The Christian Church*, p. 315.

43 Chhuanga, *An Zirtirnate*, p. v.

notion of the justice of God which inspired faith to look beyond this world and thus, to live in hope. For Christians, this hope is rooted in the death and resurrection of Jesus Christ. And this hope looks forward to the second coming of Christ that will be followed by the resurrection of the dead and the final judgment. This eschatological hope is "more a matter of promise than of prediction, and relates to eternity more than to the chronological future."[44] And as George Hendry states:

> Christian hope is not founded on specific predictions or previews of things to come, which are to be found in the Bible ...it is founded on faith in Christ....Christian hope is not really directed to "things to come," but to "Him who is to come'; and, having that assurance, it does not demand a detailed specification of the things that will happen at his coming.[45]

But, on this side of the *eschaton*, Christian faith tends to stray from "Him who is to come" and dwell on "things to come." As Webster observed, once the Christological character of eschatology declined, "the space so vacated is filled with all manner of substitutes."[46] And particularly during the medieval times, expectation of the last judgment becomes a "threatening and intimidating message" that "disseminated fear and terror in order that tempted men and women should seek comfort and salvation in the means of grace provided by the church."[47] Reviewing the ecclesiastical art of that period, Brandon noticed that for the artists, it was more demanding to depict "the joys of Heaven than the torments of Hell. This is not surprising, since

44 Fraser Watts, "Subjective and Objective Hope," in *The End of the World and the Ends of God*, ed. by John Polkinghorne and Michael Welker, (Pennsylvania: Trinity Press International, 2000), p. 48. Hereafter cited as Watts, "Subjective and Objective Hope".

45 George S. Hendry, *The Westminster Confession for Today*, (London: SCM Press Ltd., 1960), pp. 243-4. Hereafter cited as Hendry, *Westminster Confession for Today.*

46 Webster, *Word and Church*, p. 275.

47 Moltman, *Coming of God*, p. 235.

spiritual beatitude is harder to conceive than the physical sufferings of the damned."[48]

Perhaps, we can interpose this remark and relate it to the Mizo context. The threat of punishment and suffering always loomed large in Mizo concept of judgment from their first contact with the Christian missionaries till today. Influenced by their preconception of the afterlife and their harsh existential reality, the early Christians feared eternal torment in hell. Accordingly, all the subsequent theological developments we have seen partially relate to how they can escape this impending suffering. And we can say that it was their obsession with hell, as much as their longing for heaven, which kept them preoccupied with the signs of times and things to come. Thus, for many Mizo Christians, the concept of the final judgment was deprived of the hopeful anticipation of the second coming of Christ, and became a source of anxiety and fear, and even of a manipulative control mechanism.

But, it was against this kind of paralyzing and intimidating notion of judgment[49] that the Reformers preached the doctrine of "justification by faith." As a result, after the discovery of the Gospel of "justification by faith alone" Luther states that the severity of God's judgment must be held together with the kindness of God's mercy. Luther says:

> On no condition is sin a passing phase, but we are justified daily by the unmerited forgiveness of sins and by the justification of God's mercy. Sin remains, then, perpetually in this life, until

---

48 Brandon, *Judgment of the Death,* p. 127.

49 Recalling how Luther's conscience was troubled by the fear of judgment, James Dunn writes

> Luther's problem had been the mediaeval Church's emphasis on God or Christ as judge. The whole of life on earth was but a preparation for that final court of judgment, presided over by the judge of all the world, which would settle where each person spent eternity.

James D. G. Dunn and Alan M. Suggate, *The Justice of God: A Fresh Look at the Old Doctrine of Justification by Faith,* (Michigan: William. B. Eerdmans Publishing Co., 1993), pp. 7-8.

> the hour of the last judgment comes and then at last we shall be made perfectly righteous.[50]

Likewise, Calvin describes the sufficiency of Christ for the believers as follows:

> No mean assurance, this - that we shall be brought before no other judgment seat than that of our Redeemer, to whom we must look for our salvation! Moreover, he who now promises eternal blessedness through the gospel will then fulfill his promise in judgment....[T]he Father has honored [Jesus] to the end that he may care for the consciences of his people, who tremble in dread of judgment.[51]

Therefore, the "last judgment" is actually the completion of justification that "will liberate lived lives from sin and open them up to their yet-unrealized potentialities."[52] And we will not be judged by "some impossible divine standard, but by One who himself participated in it and knows what it is, from the inside."[53]

With this assurance, Mizo Christians need to "reclaim" the concept of the "last judgment" from being an anxious "process of investigation to determine the guilt or innocence of those judged"[54] to setting "all your hope on the grace that Jesus Christ will bring you when he is revealed" (2 Pet 1:13). When obsession with "specific predictions or previews of things to come" that fear often generates will be surmounted with the assurance of God's promise in Christ, eschatology and indeed, judgment will symbolize hope that even

50 Martin Luther, "The Disputation Concerning Justification," trans. and ed. by Lewis W. Spitz, in *Luther's Works,* Vol. 34, (Philadelphia: Muhlenberg Press, 1960), p. 167; cf. Martin Luther, "Against Latomus," trans. by George Lindbeck, in *Luther's Works,* Vol. 32, ed. by George W. Forell, (Philadelphia: Muhlenberg Press, 1958), p. 213.

51 Calvin, *Institutes,* II.16.18, p. 526.

52 Miroslav Volf, "Enter into Joy! Sin, Death and the Life of the World to Come," in *The End of the World and the Ends of God,* ed. by John Polkinghorne and Michael Welker, (Pennsylvania: Trinity Press International, 2000), p. 260. Hereafter cited as Volf, "Enter into Joy!"

53 Hendry, *Westminster Confession for Today,* p. 250.

54 Venema, *Promise of the Future,* p. 396.

transcended death. And as Moltmann says, hope for the coming of Christ can truly surpass fear and terror that even "the end of the world" may evoke.[55]

5.3.2. Reaffirming "judgment" as the basis for Christian accountability: Interpreting the concept of "judgment" as the culmination of God's grace upon the believers posed another problem regarding morality and responsibility in the Mizo Christian context.[56] Thus, the concept of "judgment" also needs reaffirmation.

Polkinghorne says that judgment "is the acknowledgement of moral seriousness."[57] Jesus begins his ministry by making a call to repentance because of the seriousness of sin and of God's judgment on it. The seriousness of this judgment shows that we are held accountable for our deeds. Paul recaps the key elements of the doctrine of final judgment when he writes: "For we must all appear before the Judgment seat of Christ, so that each one may receive good or evil, according to what he has done in the body" (II Cor. 5:10).

Given the inevitability of judgment, what will the nature of judgment be? Miroslav Volf maintains that thinking of the judgment of grace as a lenient judgment would be a mistake. He envisions the Day of Judgment as the day when the sins of every person "will be narrated in their full magnitude."[58] According to Terrence Nichols, standing before God in the last judgment can be a painful encounter with reality (1 Cor. 3:11-15):

> Judgment is...seeing ourselves and our whole lives as we really are....[I]t is seeing ourselves in the context of God's love, which is also truth. For most of us, this will be both joyful and painful, liberating and surprising, because encountering God's love, as

55 Moltmann, *Coming of God*, p. 232.

56 In chapter three, we have mentioned that the doctrine of "justification by faith" was stressed to the detriment of work so that Christian duty was downplayed altogether. In some case, this resulted in an antinomian tendency and some considered justification as rendering them beyond any judgment.

57 Polkinghorne, *The God of Hope*, p. 129.

58 Miroslav Volf, "The Final Reconciliation," in *Theology and Eschatology at the turn of the Millenium*, ed. by James Buckley and L. Gregory Jones, (Malden: Blackwell Publishers Ltd., 2001), p. 100.

> expressed in Jesus, will reveal all those occasions in our own lives when we fell short of love, as well as those occasions when we responded with love.[59]

These thoughts were in line with Calvin's notion of the "last judgment":

> [I]t will be a very severe test, which will penetrate to the most hidden thoughts of the heart...This will compel the lurking and lagging conscience to utter all things that have now even been forgotten.[60]

While we can see that Calvin always affirms the seriousness of the "last judgment," we also need to see his concept of "judgment" and "justification by faith" in its proper context. Calvin insists that without the grace of God, there would be no human work that would deserve justification when it was examined by God's stern judgment. But once a person, knowing that Christ is the sole means of attaining salvation, accepts Christ in faith, he/she receives a "double grace". This is reconciliation to God through Christ's blamelessness so that "we may have in heaven instead of a Judge a gracious Father; and [being] sanctified by Christ's spirit we may cultivate blamelessness and purity of life."[61]

Calvin further differentiates between God's vengeance on the ungodly "when punishment is joined with [God's] indignation" with the judgment of chastisement for the believers which aims at "correction and admonition" that "led to repentance."

> [T]he wicked groan under his scourges, yet because they do not weigh the case, [they] turn their backs on both their sins and the judgment of God....But believers, admonished by God's scourges, immediately descend into themselves to consider their sins, and struck with fear and dread, flee to prayer as suppliants for pardon. [62]

---

59 Nichols, *Death and Afterlife*, p. 161.

60 Calvin, *Institutes,* III.12.4, p. 758.

61 Calvin, *Institutes* III.11.1, p. 725.

62 Calvin, *Institutes,* III.4.31, 33, pp. 659, 662.

Therefore, the last judgment, being God's retribution upon the "unrepentant sinners," will be dreadful for them while for the believers, it will be a blessed moment of acknowledgment because of their obedience to God. And Calvin envisions this judgment within the larger context of the second coming of Christ and resurrection of the dead.

Calvin believes in the "double outcome" of the last judgment and describes the goal of resurrection as eternal enjoyment of God's presence while the fate of the ungodly is "to be cut off from all fellowship with God."[63] But, it must be noted that he strongly insists upon the inadequacy of human mental capacity to describe the mystery of heaven and the gravity of God's punishment against the wicked and warns against the "desire to know more than is lawful."[64] Calvin was mainly concerned with calming the conscience of believers from anxiety and fear of the final judgment while encouraging them to lead a responsible Christian life. Thus, in relating the concept of "the final judgment" with "justification by faith," the privileges and responsibilities of the believers must be upheld simultaneously.

5.4 Challenges of the PCI Confession of Faith Article X for Contemporary Mizo Christian Spirituality

So far, we have analyzed Article X from different aspects and enquired how various eschatological themes would be held in complement with soteriology. Now, we shall look at some challenges that Article X poses to contemporary Mizo Christian spirituality.

5.4.1. Affirming eschatology as the culmination of the Christ event in a pluralistic context: We had mentioned that Christian hope was based on the matrix of the Christ event. As R. B. Hays argues, the death of Jesus cannot be interpret only as a "propitiatory sacrifice for the forgiveness of sins of individuals" but must be placed within the broader apocalyptic account of God's final victory over evil and

63 Calvin held that the ungodly will be resurrected for judgment "to be punished for their obstinacy" while the just will be raised up "not only to eternal life but a special reward for each." Calvin, *Institutes,* III.25.9, 10, pp. 1004, 1006.

64 Calvin, *Institutes,* III.25.10, 12, pp. 1004-5, 1007-8.

death.[65] And as Ted Peters says, "Without the consummation of this transformatory promise, the Christian faith is in vain."[66] Therefore, eschatology affirms the crux of the Christian faith which anticipates the culmination of salvation in the Christ event when the power of God's triumph over evil and death will be manifested in its fullness (Phi 2:9-11).

The presence of people of other faiths and their concept of salvation pose a great challenge to Mizo Christian spirituality as their general understanding is that "there is salvation in no one else…by which we must be saved" (Acts 4:12). From the moment they became Christians, their zeal to spread the Gospel was remarkable. "Christian mission" is generally understood as "saving of the lost souls" and much effort was spent for converting "unbelievers" to Christianity. This zeal was partly inspired by the affirmation in Article X: "the unbelieving…being condemned, shall suffer the punishment due to their sin."

Hence, as Mizo Christians interact with people of other faiths, it is a great challenge to appreciate and relate meaningfully with them while maintaining the centrality of Christ and anticipating the culmination of the Christ event in the Last Day. Here, the openness of the future as well as the "provisionality" of Christian knowledge about the Last Day must be reasserted to have a reverential, and not a "condemnatory" or reactive or provocative, attitude to people of other faiths, especially in the pluralistic context of India.

5.4.2. Interpreting eschatology as the basis of ecumenism: We have seen that stressing on particular eschatological themes like "the millennial reign of Christ" and "tribulation," often caused divisions among the Mizo Christians. But, Christians ultimately share one hope: the summing up of all things in Christ (Eph 1:10). Therefore, as the Presbyterian families in India unite among themselves and with other denominational churches by sacrificing certain "distinctive" tenets in their particular doctrinal confessions, Mizo Christians are challenged to unite and come together by forsaking certain "divisive" concepts and focus on the shared hope. Likewise, Mizo Christians

65 Richard B. Hays, "Why do you Stand…," p. 124.

66 Ted Peters, "What is to come," p. viii.

are challenged to widen their eschatological imagination beyond the confines of "the Church doctrines and teachings" and learn to embrace and accommodate concepts that capture the popular eschatological imagination. Perhaps, an "inclusivistic" eschatological imagination can develop when the focus is on "the one to come", and conversely, in striving for the fulfillment of the petition of "the one to come" which is, "that they may all be one" (John 17:20). As eschatology envisioned "the summing up of all things in Christ, things in the heavens and things on the earth" (Eph 1:10; cf. 4:13), Mizo Christians are faced with a challenge to live out this eschatological vision while being here on earth.

5.4.3. Eschatology and the accountability of believers: As we looked at the privilege that believers enjoy by being justified through God's grace, we had mentioned that responsibility was laid upon believers that cannot be neglected. This responsibility was expressed as a call to obedience in Article X which states, "Those who believe in Christ and obey Him shall be openly acquitted and received into glory."[67] As Hendry rightly remarks, although we cannot be justified by our works before the judgment of God, "it is by our work that we show the reality of our faith in the saving grace of God."[68]

But showing the "reality" of their faith through their works is perhaps one of the biggest challenges facing Mizo Christians today. And the issue of corruption, understood as "the abuse of public power for private benefit"[69] can be one good example. According to Zairema, the ideal guiding pre-Christian Mizo society was the saying, *sem sem, dam dam; ei bil, thi thi,*[70] which can roughly be translated as "Share and live, withhold and die". It means that those who accumulate

---

67 This recalls the word of Calvin who writes, "Ever since both our souls and bodies were destined for heavenly incorruption and an unfading crown, we ought to strive manfully (sic) to keep them pure and uncorrupted until the Day of the Lord." Calvin, *Institutes*, III, 4.3, p. 687.

68 Hendry, *Westminster Confession for Today*, p. 251.

69 Frank R. Gunter, "Corruption," in *Encyclopedia of Social Problems*, Vol. 1, ed. by Vincent N. Parrillo, (California: SAGE Publications, Inc., 2008), p. 172.

70 Zairema, "Corruption leh Mizo Society," in *Thukhawchang Mi Pekte Hi*, comp. and ed. by Zairema and Chuathuama, (Aizawl: Zorun Community, 2009), p. 365. Hereafter cited as Zairema, *Thukhawchang Mi Pekte.*

for themselves were considered accursed[71] while generosity was considered blessedness. In fact, generosity was the impetus behind the practice of *thangchhuah* and the promise of *pialral*. And the gap between the rich and the poor was quite marginal when the Mizo society abided by this principle.

But, given the present state of affairs in Mizoram, their deviation from this ideal is very obvious. Today, great amount of budget allotted for development has failed to reach the intended target due to corrupt officials. Thanzauva even assumes that 75% of the funds allocated for development could not reach the target group.[72] Without going into further detail, an important question to pose is why the ideal of pre-Christian Mizo society that promotes sharing and generosity has been overtaken by the desire to misuse public power for private gains? Zairema remarks:

> Though we emphasized our religious experience of being born-again, this does not check corruption. As the fear of evil spirits waned, so is our censure of selfishness and greed.[73]

> Why has corruption become so prevalent in our society despite the fact that we are all Christians? Is it because we do not identify the point in which the salvation of God has to touch our live or has our interpretation leading us astray? Our preaching of the salvation of God has to be relevant to make it effective in our lives.[74]

Likewise, Vanneihtluanga believes that Mizo Christians need to be guided by the fear of God to negate corruption. He says, "We

71 Zairema, "Mizoten ei ruk kan ngaihdan," in *Thukhawchang Mi Pekte,* p. 433.

72 K. Thanzauva, *Transforming Theology: A Theological basis for Social Transformation*, (Bangalore: Asian Trading Corp., 2002), p. 104.

73 Zairema, "Mizoten ei ruk kan ngaihdan," in *Thukhawchang Mi Pekte,* p. 437.

74 Zairema, "A Quest for Indigenous Expression of Christian Theology in Mizoram," in *Ground Work for Tribal Theology in the Mizo Context*, eds. by Rosiamliana Tochhawng, K. Lalrinmawia, L. H. Rawsea, (Delhi: ISPCK, 2007), p.126. Hereafter cited as *Ground Work for Tribal Theology.*

preached too much about the God who forgives sins and now it is high time to stress that God hates and punishes sins."[75]

Therefore, maintaining the balance between privilege and responsibility of believers is a challenge to contemporary Mizo spirituality. And in the face of this challenge, the Church needs to fulfill the prophetic role of critiquing the society by insisting on the inevitability of the last judgment, which would be the "public disclosure of our allegiance to Christ and the degree of our response to that allegiance,"[76] thereby constantly reminding her members of the seriousness of every action in life. Thus, the expectation of judgment must "influence Christians in their daily living as a criterion by which to order their present life, as a summons to their conscience, and at the same time as hope in God's Justice."[77]

5.4.4. General Eschatology as a critique of individualism: In continuation with the above point, the concept of final judgment and social responsibility must be related meaningfully. Here, the challenge is to have a relevant concept of general eschatology as a critique of individualism which negates social responsibility. Josh McIntosh states that there is no hope of a resurrection of the dead in the eschatology of traditional religions, as there is no concept of a history of salvation.[78] This reflection can be connected with our previous observation that in Mizo Christian eschatology, hope for a state of spiritual bliss soon after dead was stronger than hope for a bodily resurrection in some remote future. Although personal eschatology may be a characteristic feature of Mizo eschatology, developing a vision of cosmic eschatology which is rooted in pre-Christian Mizo

---

75 Vanneihtluanga, "Nun Dawngdah leh Hlemhletna," in *Zonunmawi,* ed. and compiled by K. Thanzauva, (Aizawl: Greenhill Development and Research, 2012), p. 108.

76 Schwarz, *Eschatology,* p. 393.

77 Paul O'Callaghan, *Christ Our Hope: An Introduction to Eschatology*, (Washington, D. C.: The Catholic University of America Press, 2011), p. 130.

78 Josh McIntosh, "Relations between Creation, Redemption and Consummation in Protestant Systematic Theology," in *Hope does not Disappoint: Studies in Eschatology-Essays from Different Context*, ed. by Jochen Eber, (Bangalore: Theological Book Trust, 2001), p. 116.

ethos and not just a Judeo-Christian concept, is needed for a critique of the increasing individualism in Mizo society.

Nicholas Wolterstorff observes that a modern society is characterized by "possessive individualism...[which] demotes the giving self and promotes the grasping self, demotes the humble self and promotes the haughty self."[79] As this is just the opposite of the cherished ideal of traditional Mizo society, a modern Mizo Christian society where corruption is prevalent means that it leans toward "possessive individualism". And with the gradual decline of community bonding in Mizo society, soteriology interpreted as a purely individual affair and justification as subjective, can negate responsibility to others and to the communities. And Vanlalauva believes that this is what the current understanding of salvation and its theological theme "justification" did to Mizo society when he says, "Individualism is encouraged and individual dimension of salvation is greatly emphasized at the expense of social dimension."[80] This understanding of salvation suited an eschatological concept that is basically personal and immediate after death. And if Vanneihtluanga's argument that overstating the love of God who forgives sins resulted in disregard of corrupt practices was justified, the subjective aspect of God's love was definitely over emphasized. This promotes individualism too. Thus, the love of God for others must be reemphasized among the Mizo Christians.

This love of God was already endorsed in the Mizo ideal of *sem sem, dam dam; ei bil, thi thi*. As the road to *pialral* involves service to the community in pre-Christian Mizo eschatology, a recovery of soteriology that stressed social responsibility and communitarian service can be a genuine expression of Mizo Christian spirituality. A recovery of the Mizo ideal of *sem sem, dam dam; ei bil, thi thi* will be antithetical to corruption that wants to accumulate for oneself the share of others.

This soteriology which negates individualism and stressed social responsibility and mutual caring can be aligned with the eschatological

79 Nicholas Wolterstorff, *Justice: Rights and Wrongs*, (New Jersey: Princeton University Press, 2008), p. 3.

80 Vanlalauva, "Mizo Christian Spirituality," in *Ground Work for Tribal Theology*, p. 158.

judgment that Jesus describes in Matt 25:31-46. Calvin's teaching on "reward for believers" that we had previously described will also make sense here. This can also be related to the affirmation in Article X: "Those who have believed in Christ and obeyed Him shall be openly acquitted and received into glory." Therefore, an understanding of salvation that not only stresses individual eschatology where the goal is spiritual bliss or immortality of a spiritual soul but that looks forward to a general eschatology where believers will be "received into glory" can be a meaningful critique of individualism that creeps into the Mizo society.

General Conclusion

This thesis has attempted to analyze the discrepancies in the understanding and interpretation of the word "shall be judged according to the deeds" in relation to the understanding of the doctrine of "justification by faith." In popular Mizo Christian understanding, judgment takes place soon after death and it determines whether the departed soul will go to heaven or hell. Here, "believing God" or "justification by faith" was commonly understood as the determining factor of whether one will "go to heaven."

But, the PCI Confession of Faith was silent upon this "popular" personal eschatology while it affirms a general eschatology which was a relatively new concept in Mizo eschatological imagination. So, when this individual or personal eschatology was seen within the larger framework of the Last Day of resurrection and final judgment, it caused a tension with the understanding of salvation attained through justification by faith. Particularly, when the final judgment was portrayed almost like a fact-finding process, it caused anxiety and discomfort in the mind of the believers. Therefore, one will usually stress either God's forgiveness of sinners or the harshness of God's punishment on sinners.

After analyzing the concept of "justification by faith" and the "final judgment," this book asserts that the final judgment is the culmination of the process of justification for believers. Thus, the tension between "justification by faith" and the "final judgment" is the result of isolating and compartmentalizing these two concepts which must actually complement each other. This observation contends that eschatology and soteriology determine each other and cannot be apprehended in isolation. It also contends that eschatology as professed in Article X of the PCI Confession needs to be connected with Christology that will throw light upon the basis of Christian hope.

The implication of this insight for the present is that salvation must not be seen solely as "the saving of souls" or "going to heaven" in the afterlife. Salvation means responding to Jesus' call of repentance due to the seriousness of sin and of God's judgment on it, and living a new life in the light of Jesus' teaching. It involves a life-long process of growing in the likeness of, and witnessing for, Christ till one reaches its consummation and perfection in the Last Day. And from this perspective, the final judgment basing on "the deeds done in the present life" can be, on the one hand, a hope for an open acquittal of believers who, though not perfect, live a life of obedience to Christ, and on the other hand, the condemnation of the "unbelieving and wicked" who "shall suffer the punishment due to their sins." Therefore, the promise of God which will culminate in the Last Day can be the basis of hope that should calm the conscience of believers from anxiety and fear of the final judgment while encouraging them to lead a responsible Christian life.

A relevant contextual expression and application of the insight that justification by faith and the final judgment are interconnected involves more than an exposition of the basis of the Confession of Faith, particularly as found in Calvin's *Institutes*. A concept of "justification by faith" and "final judgment" relevant for the Mizo context involves connecting these notions with traditional norms, ideals and beliefs that we find in pre-Christian Mizo system of belief. A meaningful interface between doctrinal exposition and Mizo ideals could be a fruitful collaboration in developing a genuine Mizo Christian spirituality. And a relevant Mizo Christian eschatological imagination should be a meaningful convergence between personal eschatology and general eschatology.

Above all, a relevant Mizo Christian eschatological imagination cannot be limited to its root in the past – be it confessions or traditions. Due to the growth of knowledge through higher education coupled with the ease of interconnection and dissemination of information, current scientific perspectives of the cosmos must be especially taken into account. This will help Mizo Christian imagination to transcend its narrow confinement which tends to connect every local event with an eschatological "signs of the times". This openness to scientific perspectives must be maintained in a healthy relationship with the Christian hope which focuses on the promises of God in Jesus Christ that will be actualized through the power of the Holy Spirit. To have this holistic vision of reality through a meaningful "fusion of horizons" – drawing from the past and current insights to imagine the future so that the present makes perfect sense – is the present task of theology in the Mizo Christian context.

Appendix

Selected articles from the Twelve Articles of the "Confession of Faith of the Presbyterian Church in India" compared with the relevant corresponding words of the "Shorter Catechism" and "Larger Catechism" of the Westminster Confession of Faith and the "Summary of Principles".

Article I: The Scriptures of the Old and New Testaments are the Word of God, and the only infallible rule of faith and duty.

The Shorter Catechism: The Word of God which is contained in the Scriptures of the Old and New Testaments is the only rule to direct us how we may glorify and enjoy him.

The Larger Catechism: The holy Scriptures of the Old and New Testaments are the Word of God, the only rule of faith and obedience.

Summary of Principles: The Scriptures of the Old and New Testament are proved to be the word of God... and nothing is of authority in religion except what is either taught in them in express terms, or may he deduced from them by necessary inference.

Article II: There is but one God, and He alone is to be worshipped. He is a Spirit, self-existent, omnipresent yet distinct from all other spirits and from all material things ; infinite, eternal, and unchangeable in His being, wisdom, power, holiness, justice, goodness, truth and love.

The Shorter Catechism: God is a Spirit, infinite, eternal, and unchangeable, in his being, wisdom, power, holiness, justice, goodness and truth.

The Larger Catechism: God is a Spirit, in and of himself infinite in being, glory, blessedness, and perfection; all sufficient, eternal, unchangeable, incomprehensible, everywhere present, almighty, knowing all things, most wise, most holy, most just, most merciful and gracious, long suffering, and abundant in goodness and truth.

Summary of Principles: There is one God, the only living and true God, a spirit, infinite, eternal, independent, and unchangeable in his being, and in his power, knowledge, wisdom, holiness, justice, goodness and truth; the creator, preserver, proprietor, and governor of all things; and the sole object of worship.

Article III: In the Godhead there are three Persons, the Father, the Son, and the Holy Spirit, and these three are one God, the same in substance, equal in power and glory.

The Shorter Catechism: There are three Persons in the Godhead: the Father, the Son, and the Holy Ghost; and these three are one God, the same in substance, equal in power and glory.

The Larger Catechism: There are three persons in the Godhead: the Father, the Son, and the Holy Ghost; and these three are one true, eternal God, the same in substance, equal in power and glory, although distinguished by their personal properties.

Summary of Principles: In the Godhead there are Three Persons, - the Father, the Son and the Holy Ghost, - in essence one, and in all divine perfections equal, but each possessing a distinct personality indicated by appropriate personal names and acts.

Article IV: All things visible and invisible were created by God by the word of His power, and are so preserved and governed by Him, that while He is no way the author of sin, He worketh all things according to the counsel of His will, and they serve the fulfilment of His wise and good and holy purposes.

Summary of Principles: God, in the exercise of his holy, wise, and sovereign will, and for the manifestation of his own perfections, formed, in eternity, the plan according to which all things come to pass: "yet so as thereby neither is God the author of sin, nor is violence offered to the will of the creatures."

Article V: God created man, male and female, after His own image, in knowledge, righteousness, and holiness, with dominion over the creatures. All men have the same origin, and are brethren.

The Shorter Catechism: God created man male and female, after his own image, in knowledge, righteousness, and holiness, with dominion over the creatures.

Article VI: Our first parents, being free to choose between good and evil, and being tempted, sinned against God; and all mankind descending by ordinary generation from Adam, the head of the race, sinned in him and fell with him. To their original guilt and corruption, those capable of so doing have added actual transgressions. All justly deserve His wrath and punishment in this present life and in that which is to come.

The Larger Catechism: Our first parents, being left to the freedom of their own will, through the temptation of Satan, transgressed the commandment of God...The covenant being made with Adam, as a public person, not for himself only, but for his posterity, all mankind, descending from him by ordinary generation, sinned in him, and fell with him in that first transgression.

Summary of Principles: Our First Parents...were fully capable of yielding perfect obedience, but abusing their freedom of will, through the temptation of the devil ...forfeited the blessings implied in the Covenant, incurred its penalty, and became guilty, depraved, and miserable.

As in the Covenant, Adam was constituted the head and representative of the entire race, all his natural posterity come into the world subject to the penal consequences of his sin…and as soon as they are capable of using their moral faculties, they, by actual transgression, increase their guilt and depravity…so that, if divine mercy do not interpose, they must…die under the curse, and endure the pains of hell to all eternity.

Article VII: To save men from the guilt, corruption, and penalty of sin, and to give them eternal life, God in His infinite love sent into the world His eternal and only-begotten Son, the Lord Jesus Christ, in whom alone God has become incarnate and through whom alone men can be saved. The eternal Son became true man and so was and continueth to be true God and true man, in two distinct natures and one person for ever. He was conceived by the power of the Holy Spirit and born of the Virgin Mary, yet without sin. For sinful men He perfectly obeyed the law of God, and offered Himself a true and perfect sacrifice to satisfy divine justice and reconcile men to God. He died on the cross, was buried, and rose again from the dead on the third day. He ascended to the right hand of God, where He maketh intercession for His people, and whence He shall come again to raise the dead and to judge the world.

Summary of Principles: God foreseeing the fall of man, in sovereign mercy…formed an arrangement…whereby sin might be atoned for, salvation freely offered to sinners, and that salvation secured to all who had been the objects of his electing love. For these ends the Son of God was constituted the Mediator between God and man…and the "Saviour of the world." When the appointed time arrived, He took into union with his own divine person, a perfect human nature, and became Man, being conceived by the power of the Holy Ghost in the womb of a virgin, and born of her, yet without sin. Being made under the law which man had broken, He yielded perfect obedience to it, and so far as was consistent with his absolute holiness, endured its penalty both in his life of suffering, and in his death upon the cross. The dignity of his person rendered his obedience unto death infinitely meritorious, and thus a fit ground on which all who believe on his name are justified and receive the Holy Spirit, to the glory of God's righteousness as well as of his grace.

In testimony of the acceptance of the Saviour's work by the Father, He was raised from the dead, and received up into Heaven, where, in virtue of his sacrifice, He, as the great High Priest, makes intercession for his people, and, as Lord of all, rules the Church and the world. At the time appointed He will come again to the earth to raise the dead, judge the world, and make his people perfectly happy with himself in heaven forever.

Article VIII: The Holy Spirit who proceedeth from the Father and the Son, maketh men partakers of salvation, convincing them of their sin and misery, enlightening their minds in the knowledge of Christ, renewing their wills, persuading and enabling them to embrace Jesus Christ, freely offered to them in the Gospel, and working in them all the fruits of righteousness.

The Shorter Catechism: Effectual calling is the work of God's Spirit, whereby, convincing us of our sin and misery, enlightening our minds in the knowledge of Christ, and renewing our wills, he doth persuade and enable us to embrace Jesus Christ, freely offered to us in the gospel.

The Larger Catechism: Effectual calling is the work of God's almighty power and grace, whereby...he doth in his accepted time invite and draw them to Jesus Christ, by his Word and Spirit; savingly enlightening their minds, renewing and powerfully determining their wills, so as they...are hereby made willing and able, freely to answer his call, and to accept and embrace the grace offered and conveyed therein.

Summary of Principles: In the gospel the Lord Jesus Christ is exhibited as the Saviour of sinners...But it is only when the sinner, by the agency of the Holy Spirit—who is promised to all who ask Him—and through the instrumentality of the word, has been convinced of his sin and misery, and has had his mind enlightened in the knowledge of Christ, and his will renewed, that he, through the faith of the gospel, receives Jesus Christ as his own Saviour, and so enters on the enjoyment of the salvation procured by Him, and made known in the gospel.

Article IX: While God chose a people in Christ before the foundation of the world, that they should be holy and without blemish before Him in love; having foreordained them unto adoption as sons through Jesus Christ unto Himself, according to the good pleasure of His will, to the praise of the glory of His grace, which He freely bestowed on them in the Beloved; He maketh a full and free offer of salvation to all men, and commandeth them to repent of their sins, to believe in the Lord Jesus Christ as their Saviour, and to live a humble and holy life after His example and in obedience to God's revealed will. Those who believe in Christ and obey Him are saved, the chief benefits which they receive being justification, adoption into the number of the sons of God, sanctification through the indwelling of the Spirit, and eternal glory. Believers may also in this life enjoy assurance of their salvation. In His gracious work the Holy Spirit useth the means of grace, especially the word, sacraments, and prayer.

Summary of Principles: United to Christ by faith, the believer has a personal interest in his righteousness, and is pardoned, and accepted as righteous by God; and the work of sanctification begun in conversion is carried on by the continued operation of the Holy Ghost, through faith, so that the believer is preserved, strengthened, and comforted, till he is prepared for heaven.

The internal means of salvation are exercises of the mind and heart, produced by the operation of the Holy Ghost through the instrumentality of the word...The external means of salvation are the Word read or preached, prayer, and other divinely instituted ordinances of religion.

Article X: The sacraments instituted by Christ are Baptism and the Lord's Supper. Baptism is the washing with water in the name of the Father and of the Son and of the Holy Spirit, and is a sign and seal of our union to Christ, of regeneration and renewing of the Holy Spirit, and of our engagement to be the Lord's. It is to be administered to those who profess their faith in Christ and to their children. The Lord's Supper is the partaking of the bread and of the cup as a memorial of Christ's death and is a sign and seal of the benefits thereof to believers. It is to be observed by His people till

He come, in token of their faith in Him and His sacrifice, of their appropriation of its benefits, of their further engagement to servo Him, and of their communion with Him and with one another. The benefits of the sacraments are not from any virtue in them, or in him that doth administer them, but only from the blessing of Christ and the working of His Spirit in them that by faith receive them.

The Shorter Catechism: A sacrament is a holy ordinance instituted by Christ, wherein, by sensible signs, Christ and the benefits of the new covenant are represented, sealed, and applied to the believers.

The sacraments of the New Testament are Baptism and the Lord's Supper.

Baptism is a sacrament, wherein the washing with water, in the name of the Father, and of the Son, and of the Holy Ghost, doth signify and seal our ingrafting into Christ, and partaking of the benefits of the covenant of grace, and our engagement to be the Lord's.

The Lord's Supper is a sacrament, wherein by giving and receiving bread and wine, according to Christ's appointment, his death is showed forth.

Summary of Principles: [T]here are two emblematical institutions usually termed Sacraments, — baptism and the Lord's Supper. In those, by outward signs, spiritual truths are represented and confirmed— the fundamental principles of Christianity and their evidence are brought before the mind, and thus, "by the blessing of God, and the working of his Spirit," spiritual benefit is conferred on "those who by faith receive them."

In Baptism the application of water to the body symbolizes the truth —"that men are purified from sin — freed from guilt and depravity, by the atonement of Christ and the influence of the Holy Spirit," and the person baptized is recognized as connected with the visible church. The ordinance is to be administered to unbaptized adults on their making a credible profession of their faith in Christ, and their obedience to him: and to the infants of such as are members of the church.

In the Lord's Supper, by the distribution and use of bread broken and wine poured out, are represented and confirmed the truths, — "that Jesus Christ, the Son of God, in human nature, suffered and died in the room of men, to obtain their pardon and salvation —that in the faith of these truths men enjoy the benefits procured by his death — that all who believe are united in a holy fellowship, and bound to yield implicit obedience to all Christ's laws;" and the believing participants of "the bread" and of "the cup" have communion with Christ, and partake of the benefits of his salvation, "to their spiritual nourishment and growth in grace." The Lord's Supper is therefore to be observed by believers as a memorial of Christ's sacrificial death, as a public profession of their faith in Him and subjection to his authority, and as an expression of the communion which they have with Him and with one another. As it must be profaned if observed in ignorance and unbelief, or in the allowed practice of sin, serious self-examination ought to precede the service, and it ought to be performed in the exercise of faith, love, repentance, and self-dedication to God.

Article XI: It is the duty of all believers to unite in Church fellowship, to observe the sacraments and other ordinances of Christ, to obey His laws, to continue in prayer, to keep holy the Lord's Day, to meet together for His worship, to wait upon the preaching of His word, to give as God may prosper them, to manifest a Christlike spirit among themselves and towards all men, to labour for the extension of Christ's kingdom throughout the world, and to wait for His glorious appearing.

Summary of Principles: On the first day of the week...Christians are to come together to observe the ordinances of public worship: and are to devote the whole day to religious exercises, "except so much as is to be taken up in the works of necessity and mercy."

These ordinances of public worship are the teaching of Christian truth, the offering up of prayers and praises to God in the name of Jesus Christ, and the "fellowship" or communication of their property by the members of the Church, as God has prospered them, for maintaining and extending the cause of Christ.

(Sources: "Confession of Faith and Constitution of the Presbyterian Church in India" in *Report of Commission II: The Church in the Mission Field.* Edinburgh: World Missionary Conference, 1910, pp.297-9; "The Shorter Catechism" and "The Larger Catechism" in *The Constitution of the Presbyterian Church (U.S.A.): Part I – Book of Confessions.* Louisville: The Office of the General Assembly, *Presbyterian Church (U.S.A.),* 1996, pp.179-252; *Summary of Principles of the United Presbyterian Church (Scotland).* Toronto: Charles Fletcher, 1856, pp.7-11).

Bibliography

I. Books

Althaus, Paul. *The Theology of Martin Luther.* Philadelphia: Fortress Press, 1981.

Anderson, H. John., T. A. Murphy and Joseph A. Burgess, eds. *Justification by Faith: Lutheran and Catholics in Dialogue VII.* Minneapolis: Augsburg Publishing House, 1985.

Assembly of the Presbyterian Church in North East India Golden Jubilee Souvenir: 1926-1976. Shillong: Central Ward, 1976.

Augustine, *The City of God.* Translated by Marcus Dods. 3rd Printing Hendrickson Publishers Edition. Massachusetts: Hendrickson Publishers, Inc., 2011.

Bainton, Roland H. *Here I Stand: A Life of Martin Luther.* Tennessee: Abingdon Press, 1950.

Baird, J. Arthur. *The Justice of God in the Teaching of Jesus*. London: SCM Press Ltd., 1963.

Bauckham, Richard. *The Jewish World around the New Testament.* Tubingen: Mohr Siebeck, 2008.

Biaksiama, P. C. *666: Sakawlh leh a Chhinchhiahna*. Aizawl: Christian Research Centre, 2010.

Brandon, S. G. F. *The Judgment of the Death: The Idea of Life after Death in the Major Religions.* New York: Charles Scribner's Sons, 1967.

Calvin, John. *Institutes of the Christian Religion*. Translated by Ford Lewis Battles. Philadelphia: The Westminster Press, 1960.

Chambers, Paul. *Religion, Secularization and Social Change in Wales: Congregational Studies in a Post Christian Society*. Cardiff: University of Wales Press, 2004.

Charlesworth, J. H. *Resurrection: The Origin and Future of a Biblical Doctrine*. London: T&T Clark, 2006.

Cracknell, Kenneth. *Justice, Courtesy and Love: Theologians and Missionaries Encountering the World Religions*, 1846-1914. London: Epworth Press, 1995.

Curtis, William A. *A History of Creeds and Confessions of Faith in Christendom and Beyond.* Aberdeen: Aberdeen University, 1911.

Dales, John B. and R. M. Patterson, eds. *Report of Proceedings of the Second General Council of the Presbyterian Alliance*. Philadelphia: Presbyterian Journal Company, 1880.

Daley, Brian Edward. *The Hope of the Early Church: A Handbook of Patristic Theology*. Cambridge: Cambridge University Press, 1991.

Dawkins, Richard. *River out of Eden: A Darwinian View of Life.* London: Weidenfeld & Nicolson, 1995.

Dokhuma, James. *Zoram Kohhran Tualto Chanchin.* Revised edition. Kulikawn: J. D. Press, 1997.

Drysdale, A. H. *History of the Presbyterians in England.* London: Publication Committee of the Presbyterian Church of England, 1889.

Dunn, James D. G. and Alan M. Suggate, *The Justice of God: A Fresh Look at the Old Doctrine of Justification by Faith*. Michigan: William. B. Eerdmans Publishing Co., 1993.

Frykholm, Amy Johnson. *Rapture Culture: Left Behind in Evangelical America*. Oxford: Oxford University Press, Inc., 2004.

Green, Garrett. *Theology, Hermeneutics, and Imagination: The Crisis of Interpretation at the End of Modernity*. Cambridge: Cambridge University Press, 2004.

Haar, Gerrie ter and James J. Busuttil, eds. *The Freedom to do God's Will: Religious Fundamentalism and Social Change*. New York: Routledge, 2003.

Henderson, G. D. *Presbyterianism*. Aberdeen: The University Press, 1956.

Hendry, George S. *The Westminster Confession for Today*. London: SCM Press Ltd., 1960.

Higgins, A. J. B. *The Son of Man in the Teaching of Jesus*. Cambridge: Cambridge University Press, 1980.

Hminga, C. L. *The Life and Witness of the Churches in Mizoram*. Serkawn: The Literature Society, BCM, 1987.

Inbody, Tyron. *The Faith of The Christian Church - An Introduction to Theology*. Michigan: Wm. B. Eerdmans Publishing Co., 2005.

Jones, David Ceri. *A Glorious Work in the World: Welsh Methodism and the International Evangelical Revival, 1735–1750*. Cardiff: University of Wales Press, 2004.

Jones, R. Tudur. *Faith and the Crisis of a Nation: Wales 1890–1914*. Edited by Robert Pope. Cardiff: University of Wales Press, 2004.

Kristian Hla Bu. Aizawl: SL & PB, 2004.

Kristian Tlangau Centenary Project: Kum 1911-2011 chhung atanga Editorial leh Zawhna leh Chhanna Lawrkhawm. Aizawl: SL&PB, 2011.

Lalhmuaka. *Zoram thim ata Engah*. Aizawl : SPB, 1988.

Lalmuankima, C. *Impact of Westernization on Mizo Spirituality-Implications for the Development of Relevant Christian Spirituality in Mizoram*. Bangalore: SFS Publications, 2013.

Lalruali. *Zoram Hmarchhak Harhna Chanchin*. Aizawl : SL&PB, 1997.

Lalruma. *Taksa Tlanna: Miten Pathian Ram An Beisei Dan*. Aizawl: SPB, 1985.

Lalsangliana, C. *Kohhran Thurin*. Aizawl: SL&PB, 2014.

Lalsawma. *Kristian Thurin Zirna*. Aizawl: SL&PB, 1998.

________. *Revivals – The Mizo Way*. Mission Vengthlang: Lalsawma, 1994.

Lalthangliana, B. *Pi Pu Chhuahtlang*. Aizawl: Hrangbana College, 1998.

Lewis, Grace R. *The Lushai Hills: The Story of the Lushai Pioneer Mission*. London: The Baptist Missionary Society, 1906.

Lloyd, Gareth. *Charles Wesley and the Struggle for Methodist Identity*. Oxford : Oxford University Press, 2007.

Lloyd, J. M. *History of the Church in Mizoram*. Aizawl : SPB, 1991.

Luther, Martin. “The Disputation Concerning Justification”. Translated and edited by Lewis W. Spitz. In *Luther's Works, Vol. 34*. Philadelphia: Muhlenberg Press, 1960.

____________. “Thesis Concerning Faith and Law”. Translated and edited by Lewis W. Spitz. In *Luther's Works, Vol. 34*. Philadelphia: Muhlenberg Press, 1960.

____________. “Against Latomus”. Translated by George Lindbeck. In *Luther's Works, Vol. 32*. Edited by George W. Forell. Philadelphia: Muhlenberg Press, 1958.

MacPherson, John. *The Westminster Confession of Faith with Introduction and Notes*. Edinburg: T&T Clark,1881.

Manual of Worship of the Presbyterian Church of India. Shillong: The Presbyterian Church of India, 2002.

Marby, Hunter P. *A Manual for Researchers and Writers*. 2nd ed. Bangalore: BTESSC, 2012.

McGrath, Alister E. *Christian Theology: An Introduction.* 4th ed. Malden: Blackwell Publishing, 2007.

Mendus, E. L. *The Diary of a Jungle Missionary*. Liverpool: Foreign Mission Office, 1956.

Mizo Kristian Hla Thar Bu. Aizawl: SL&PB, 2007.

Moltmann, Jurgen. *The Coming of God: Christian Eschatology*. Translated by Margaret Kohl. London: SCM Press Ltd, 1996.

Morris, John H. *The History of the Welsh Calvinistic Methodists Foreign Mission: To the End of the Year 1904*. Carnavon: The Calvinistic Methodists Bookroom, 1910.

Morris, Leon. *The Biblical Doctrine of Judgment*. London: The Tyndale Press, 1960.

Nichols, Terence. *Death and Afterlife: A Theological Introduction*. Michigan: Brazos Press, 2010.

O'Callaghan, Paul. *Christ Our Hope: An Introduction to Eschatology*. Washington, D. C.: The Catholic University of America Press, 2011.

O'Collins, Gerald. *Christology: A Biblical, Historical and Systematic Study of Christ*. 2nd ed. Oxford: Oxford University Press, 2009.

Paik, L. George. *The History of Protestant Missions in Korea, 1832-1910*. Pyongyang: Union Christian College Press, 1927.

Polkinghorne, John *Exploring Reality: The Intertwining of Science and Religion*. New Haven: Yale University Press, 2005.

_________________. *The God of Hope and the End of the World*. New Haven: Yale University Press, 2002.

Quistorp, Heinrich. *Calvin's Doctrine of the Last Things*. London: Lutterworth Press, 1955.

Radano, John A. *Lutheran and Catholic Reconciliation on Justification*. Michigan: William B. Eerdmans Pubishing Co., 2009.

Rinehart, James F. *Apocalyptic Faith and Political Violence: Prophets of Terror*. New York: Palgrave Macmillan, 2006.

Robert, Dana L. *Christian Mission: How Christianity Became a World Religion*. West Sussex: John Wiley & Sons Ltd, 2009.

Saiaithanga. *Mizo Kohhran Chanchin*. 1st ed. Aizawl: MTLC, 1969.

_________. *Thurin Zirna*, 5th rev. ed. Aizawl: SPB, 1989.

Schwarz, Hans. *Eschatology*. Michigan: William B. Eerdmans Pubishing Co., 2000.

Snaitang, O. L. *Christianity and Social Change in Northeast India*. Shillong: Vendrame Institute, 1993.

Spurgeon, C. H. *Advice for Seekers.* First Banner of Truth Edition. Edinburgh: The Banner of Truth Trust, 1993.

Summary of Principles of the United Presbyterian Church (Scotland). Toronto: Charles Fletcher, 1856.

Sundkler, Bengt. *Church of South India: The Movement Towards Union, 1900-1947*. London: Lutterworth Press, 1954.

Taylor, Mark C. *Erring: A Postmodern A/theology*. Chicago: The University of Chicago Press, 1984.

Thangzauva, K., compiler. *Reports of the Foreign Mission of the Presbyterian Church of Wales on Mizoram 1894-1957*. Aizawl: SL&PB, 1997.

Thanmawia, R. L. *Mizo Hla Hlui (Mizo Folk Songs)*. Aizawl: Mizoram Publication Board, 2012.

____________. *Transforming Theology: A Theological Basis for Social Transformation*. Bangalore: Asian Trading Corp., 2002.

The Annual Report of B.M.S on Mizoram, 1901-1938. Serkawn: Mizoram Gospel Centenary Committee, Baptist Church of Mizoram, 1993.

The Constitution of the Presbyterian Church in Assam. Aijal: The Welsh Mission Bookroom, 1925.

The Constitution of the Presbyterian Church in Assam. Aijal: The Loch Printing Press, 1955.

The Constitution of the Presbyterian Church in NE India. Shillong: The Khasi Jaintia Presbyterian Press, 1968.

The Constitution of the Presbyterian Church of India. Shillong: The Khasi Jaintia Synod Press, 1993.

The Constitution of the Presbyterian Church of India. 7th rev. ed. Shillong: The Presbyterian Church of India, 2004.

The Constitution of the Presbyterian Church, (USA): Part I - Book of Confessions. Louisville: The Office of the General Assembly, 1996.

The Faith of the Early Fathers. Volume Three. Selected and translated by William A. Jurgens. Bangalore: TPI, 1984.

The History, Constitution, Rules of Discipline and Confession of Faith of the Calvinistic Methodist in Wales, 2nd ed. Chester: Parry and Son, 1834.

The Westminster Confession of Faith and Catechisms in Modern English. 3rd ed. Michigan: Evangelical Presbyterian Church, 2010.

Tlangawia, Chawngchhuanga, Sangthanga, eds. *Kohhran Chanchin.* N.E. Khawdungsei: Presbyterian Kohhran Committee, 1994.

Tochhawng, Rosiamliana. *A Study of the Ten Articles of Faith of the Presbyterian Church in India.* Delhi: ISPCK, 2007.

Vanlalauva, H. *Hun Hnuhnung Thu: Mizoram Presbyterian Kohhran 2011 Nilai leh Beihrual Thupui.* Aizawl: SL&PB, 2010.

Vanlalchhuanawma. *Christianity and Subaltern Culture: Revival Movement as a Cultural Response to Westernisation in Mizoram.* Delhi: ISPCK, 2006.

Vanlalchhuanga. *An Zirtirnate leh an Chanchin.* Revised and enlarged. Venghnuai: Gosen Home, 2010.

Vanlalthlana. *Doctrine of Grace: Augustine's Doctrine of Grace and Human Free Will and an Appraisal from a Mizo Christian Perspective.* Delhi: ISPCK, 2010.

Venema, Cornelis P. *The Promise of the Future.* Edinburgh: The Banner of Truth Trust, 2000.

Webster, John. *Word and Church: Essays in Christian Dogmatics.* Edinburgh: T&T Clark Ltd, 2001.

Wilkinson, David. *Christian Eschatology and the Physical Universe.* London: T&T Clark International, 2010.

Williams, William. *Welsh Calvinistic Methodism: A Historical Sketch.* London: James Nisbet and Co., 1872.

______________. *Welsh Calvinistic Methodism - A Historical Sketch of the Presbyterian Church of Wales.* London: Publishing Office of the Presbyterian Church of England,1884.

Williamson, W. Paul. Ralph W. Hood, Jr., and Peter C. Hill, eds. *The Psychology of Religious Fundamentalism.* New York: The Guilford Press, 2005.

Wolterstorff, Nicholas. *Justice: Rights and Wrongs.* New Jersey: Princeton University Press, 2008.

World Missionary Conference, 1910: Report of Commission II. Edinburgh: Oliphant, Anderson and Ferrier, 1910.

Wright, N. T. *The Resurrection of the Son of God.* Minneapolis: Fortress Press, 2003.

Young, David. *The Origin and History of Methodism in the Wales and the Border.* London: Charles H. Kelly, 1893.

Zairema. *Pi Pute Biak Hi.* Edited by Chhuauthuama. Aizawl: Zorun Community, 2009.

______. *Thukhawchang Mi Pekte Hi.* Compiled and edited by Zairema and Chuathuama. Aizawl: Zorun Community, 2009.

Zawla, K. *Mizo Pi Pute leh an Thlahte Chanchin.* 3rd ed., rev. and enlarged. Aizawl: H.A. Press, 1981.

II. Chapters in Books

Aune, David E. and Eric Stewart. "From the Idealized Past to the Imagery Future: Eschatological Restoration in Jewish Apocalyptic Literature." In *Restoration: Old Testament, Jewish, and Christian Perspectives.* Edited by James M. Scott. Leiden: Brill, 2001.

Baker, Rudder Lynne "Death and the Afterlife." In *The Oxford Handbook of Philosophy of Religion.* Edited by William J. Wainwright. Oxford: Oxford University Press, 2005.

Chuauthuama. "Mizo Kristiante Hun Hnuhnung Thlir Dan." In *Calvina Zirtirna leh Mizo Nun.* Edited by Vanlalchhuanawma. Aizawl: Calvin Study Centre, ATC, 2000.

Green, Garrett. "Imagining the Future." In *The Future as God's Gift: Exploration in Christian Eschatology.* Edited by David Fergusson and Marcel Sarot. Edinburgh: T&T Clark Ltd., 2000.

Hanson, Paul D. "Prophetic and Apocalyptic politics." In *The Last Things.* Edited by C. E. Braaten and R.W. Jenson. Michigan: William B. Eerdmans Publishing Co., 2002.

Hays, Richard B. "Why do you Stand Looking Up Toward Heaven?" In *Theology and Eschatology at the Turn of the Millenium*. Edited by James Buckley and L. Gregory Jones. Malden: Blackwell Publishers Ltd., 2001.

Hughes, Kevin L. "The Crossing of Hope, or Apophatic Eschatology." In *The Future of Hope*. Edited by Miroslav Volf and William Katerberg. Michigan: William B. Eerdmans Publishing Co., 2004.

Lalbiaktluanga. "Mizorama Zirtirna Hrang Hrang Thlirna." In *Mizo Miziaa Pathian Thu*. Aizawl: SPB, 1998.

Lalsawma. "Sual leh Chhandamna Thu Mizoram Kristianten an Zirtir Dan." In *Calvina Zirtirna leh Mizo Nun*. Edited by C. Lalhlira. Aizawl: Calvin Study Centre, ATC, 2002.

McGuckin, John A. "The Book of Revelation and Orthodox Eschatology: The Theodrama of judgment." In *The Last Things*. Edited by C. E. Braaten and R.W. Jenson. Michigan: William B. Eerdmans Publishing Co., 2002.

McIntosh, Josh. "Relations between Creation, Redemption and Consummation in Protestant Systematic Theology." In *Hope does not Disappoint: Studies in Eschatology - Essays from Different Context*. Edited by Jochen Eber. Bangalore: Theological Book Trust, 2001.

Palmer, Edwin J. "Towards Unity." In *The Christian Task in India*. Edited by John McKenzie. London: MacMillan and Co., Ltd, 1929.

Pannenberg, Wolfhart. "The Task of Christian Eschatology." In *The Last Things*. Edited by C. E. Braaten and R.W. Jenson. Michigan: William B. Eerdmans Publishing Co., 2002.

Penellum, Terence. "Christianity." In *Life after Death in World Religions*. Edited by Harold Coward. Delhi: Sat Guru Publications, 1997.

Peters, Ted. "What is to come." In *Resurrection: Theological and Scientific Assessment*. Edited by Ted Peters, Robert John Russell and Michael Welker. Michigan: William B. Eerdmans Publishing Co., 2002.

Porter, Andrew. "Missions and empire, c.1873–1914." In *The Cambridge History of Christianity, Vol. 8: World Christianities, c.1815 - c.1914*. Edited by Sheridan Gilley and Brian Stanley. Cambridge: Cambridge University Press, 2006.

Schwobel, Christoph. "Last things first?" In *The Future as God's Gift: Exploration in Christian Theology*. Edited by David Fergusson and Marvel Sarot. Edinburgh: T&T Clark, 2000.

Segal, Eliezer. "Judaism." In *Life after Death in World Religions*. Edited by Harold Coward. Delhi: Sat Guru Publications, 1997.

Thanmawia, R. L. "Harhnain a hrin hla leh a phuahtute." In *Harhna: Mizoram Revival Centenary Souvenir, 1906-2006*. Aizawl: Revival Centenary Committee, 2006.

Thanzauva, K. "Sap Upa leh Pu Buanga-te Historical leh Theological Background." In *Mizorama Missionary Hmasa Ber – F. W. Savidge & J. H. Lorrain*. Edited by V.L. Hruaia Khiangte, Vanlalchhawna Khiangte, R. Zolawma. Tanhril: AICS, 2010.

Tudur, Geraint. "'Thou Bold Champion, Where art Thou?': Howell Harris and the Issue of Welsh Identity." In *Religion and National Identity, Wales and Scotland c.1700–2000*. Edited by Robert Pope. Cardiff: University of Wales Press, 2001.

Vanlalauva, H. "Mizo Christian Spirituality." In *Ground Work for Tribal Theology in the Mizo Context*. Edited by Rosiamliana Tochhawng, K. Lalrinmawia, L. H. Rawsea. Delhi: ISPCK, 2007.

Vanlallawma, C. "Sialsuk Pastor Bial Hlimsang Harhna leh a Chhehvel." In *Harhna: Mizoram Revival Centenary Souvenir, 1906-2006*. Aizawl: Revival Centenary Committee, 2006.

Vanneihtluanga. "Nun Dawngdah leh Hlemhletna." In *Zonunmawi: Mizo Nun Kawng Zawh – Danglamna, Vision, Harsatna, Nunmawi leh Hmabak*. Edited and compiled by K. Thanzauva. Aizawl: Greenhill Development and Research, 2012.

Vardy, Peter. "A Christian Approach to Eternal Life." In *Beyond Death: Theological and Philosophical Reflections on Life after Death*. Edited by Dan Cohn-Sherbok and Christopher Lewis. London: Macmillan Press Ltd., 1995.

Volf, Miroslav. "Enter into Joy! Sin, Death and the Life of the World to Come." In *The End of the World and the Ends of God.* Edited by John Polkinghorne and Michael Welker. Pennsylvania: Trinity Press International, 2000.

____________. "The Final Reconciliation." In *Theology and Eschatology at the turn of the Millenium.* Edited by James Buckley and L. Gregory Jones. Malden: Blackwell Publishers Ltd., 2001.

____________. "Retrieving Hope." In *The Future of Hope.* Edited by Miroslav Volf and William Katerberg. Michigan: Wm. B. Eerdmans Pub. Co., 2004.

Watts, Fraser. "Subjective and Objective Hope." In *The End of the World and the Ends of God.* Edited by John Polkinghorne and Michael Welker. Pennsylvania: Trinity Press International, 2000.

Zairema."A Quest for Indigenous Expression of Christian Theology in Mizoram" and "The Mizo Church." In *Ground Work for Tribal Theology in the Mizo Context.* Edited by Rosiamliana Tochhawng, K. Lalrinmawia, L. H. Rawsea. Delhi: ISPCK, 2007.

_____. "Kristian Nih Hmaa Mizo Sakhua." In *Mizo Miziaa Pathian Thu.* Aizawl: SPB, 1988.

______. "The Mizos and Their Religion." In *Towards a Tribal Theology: The Mizo Perspective.* Edited by K. Thanzauva. Mizoram: Mizo Theological Conference, 1989.

III. Entries in Encyclopaedias and Dictionaries

"United Kingdom and Ireland." In *Historical Dictionary of the Reformed Churches,* 2nd edition. Edited by Benedetto, Robert. and Donald K. McKim. Maryland: Scarecrow Press, Inc., 2010, pp. 492-8.

Gunter, Frank R. "Corruption." In *Encyclopedia of Social Problems,* Vol. 1. Edited by Vincent N. Parrillo. California: SAGE Publications, Inc., 2008, pp. 172-5.

Harvey, Van A. "Scholasticism." In *A Handbook of Theological Terms.* London: George Allen and Unwin Ltd., 1964, p. 186.

"Indulgences." In *Encyclopedia of the Renaissance and the Reformation.* Revised edition. Edited by Jennifer Speake and Thomas G. Bergin., New York: Facts On File, Inc, 2004, pp. 252-3.

Landes, Richard A. "Millennialism in the Western World." In *The Encyclopedia of Millennialism and Millennial Movements.* Edited by Richard A. Landes. New York: Routledge, 2000, pp. 453-66.

Lorrain, J. H. "Thangchhuah." In *Dictionary of the Lushai Language.* Calcutta: The Asiatic Society, 1940, p. 447.

Schultz, Richard. "Justice." In *New International Dictionary of Old Testament Theology and Exegesis,* Vol. 4. Edited by W. A. VanGemeran. Carlisle: Paternoster Press, 1996, pp. 837-46.

Whalen, Robert K. "Postmillennialism" and "Premillennialism." In *The Encyclopedia of Millennialism and Millennial Movements.* Edited by Richard A. Landes. New York: Routledge, 2000, pp. 578-83, 584-9.

IV. Articles in Newsletters, Journals and Magazines

"Chhiarpui leh Sakawlh." *Synod Newsletter,* 28/ 320, June, 2010, p. 1.

Hwang, Jae-Buhm. "The first Asian Ecumenical Confession of Faith: The So-Called Twelve Articles of Faith of Many Asian Protestant Churches." *The Ecumenical Review*, Vol. 63/2, July 2011, 200-10.

Lungmuana, K. "Merits and Demerits of Being a member of the WCC." *Presbyterian Review*, 16/52, Oct.-Dec., 2008, pp. 41-7.

Pachuau, Lalsangkima. "Mizo 'Sakhua' in Transition – Change and Continuity from Primal Religion to Christianity." *Missiology: An International Review,* 34/1, January, 2006, pp. 41-57.

Sauter, Gerhard. "The Concept and Task of Eschatology: Theological and Philosophical Reflections." In *Scottish Journal of Theology,* 41/4, Nov. 1988, pp. 499-515.

"Tunlaia Sakawlh Hlaute Thil Hlauh Hi." *Synod Newsletter,* 28/365, February, 2014, p. 1.

V. Minutes and Reports

Minutes of the First General Assembly of the Presbyterian Church in India, Allahabad, 19 December 1904.

Minutes of the Fourth General Assembly of the Presbyterian Church in India, Calcutta, 31 December 1907.

Minutes of the Ninth General Assembly of the Presbyterian Church in India, Nagpur, 28 December 1917.

Minutes of the Tenth General Assembly of the Presbyterian Church in India, Calcutta, 30 December 1919.

Minutes of the First General Assembly of the United Church of India (North), Bombay, 30 December 1924.

Minutes of the SPB Meeting, Aizawl, 22 January 1992. (Cyclostyled).

Minutes of the SPB Meeting, Aizawl, 17 November 1993. (Cyclostyled).

Minutes of the SPB Meeting, Aizawl, 18 January 1994. (Cyclostyled).

Minutes of the SL&PB Meeting, Aizawl, 2 August 1995. (Cyclostyled).

Minutes of the SL&PB Meeting, Aizawl 23 October 1995. (Cyclostyled).

Minutes of the SL&PB Meeting, Aizawl 25 July 1996. (Cyclostyled).

Minutes of the 2010 Synod Meeting, Gen. 77. Aizawl: Synod Press, 2010.

Minutes of the 2011 Synod Meeting, Gen. 44. Aizawl: Synod Press, 2011.

VI. Unpublished Materials and Interviews

Jyrwa, J. Fortiswell. *A Historical Study on the Growth and Development of the Khasi-Jaintia Presbyterian Church in the Twentieth Century.* MTh Thesis submitted to the Senate of Serampore, 1974.

Lalthanmawia, R. *Reinterpretation of Calvin in the Light of the Ten Articles of Faith of the Presbyterian Church of India.* (Unpublished).

Parker, K. L. *The Development of the United Church of Northern India.* A Dissertation submitted to the Faculty of the Divinity School in Candidacy for the Degree of Doctor of Philosophy, 1935.

"Religion," *Wales Factfile,* (Cardiff: Institute of Welsh Affairs). http://www. clickonwales.org/wp-content/uploads/6_Factfile_Religion.pdf. (15 August 2013).

Interview with Chuauthuama at Aizawl Theological College, Durtlang, 2 September 2013.

Interview with Lalsawma at his residence, Mission Vengthlang, Aizawl, 10 September 2013.

Interview with R. Lalthanmawia at his residence, Khatla, Aizawl, 14 September 2013.